"He Is Risen!"

A New Reading of Mark's Gospel

by

Hugh M. Humphrey

D1569390

Paulist Press
New York / Mahwah, N.J.

Book design by Nighthawk Design.

Library of Congress Cataloging-in-Publication Data

Humphrey, Hugh M.
    He is risen: a new reading of Mark's Gospel/by Hugh M. Humphrey.
      p.   cm.
    Includes bibliographical references and index.
    ISBN 0-8091-3302-4 (pbk.)
    1. Bible. N.T. Mark—Commentaries. I. Title.
BS2585.3.H86 1992
226.3'077—dc20   91-44459
                                                      CIP

Published by Paulist Press
997 Macarthur Boulevard
Mahwah, New Jersey 07430

Printed and bound in the
United States of America

Contents

NEW TESTAMENT PALESTINE

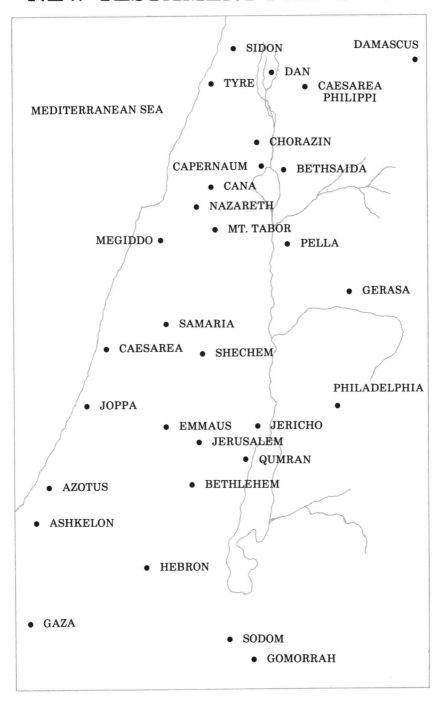

Introduction

The gospel of Mark is deceptive. Shorter than the other gospels, simple in expression and lacking most of the sayings of Jesus which can be used so effectively to establish ethical or ecclesial positions, Mark is nonetheless as fine a statement of what is the fundamental and distinguishing feature of Christianity as any of the most elaborate theological treatises over the centuries. But Mark doesn't appear to be that, and therein lies its deceptive quality. Because on the surface this gospel tells the story of Jesus, we read it too often looking for that historical material which will inform us about the Jesus of Nazareth. We are not accustomed to attend to a "story" for its "meaning" or "theology" (as we would call it today), but that is what Mark asked of his audience and that is what this book seeks to present: an interpretive reading of the gospel of Mark which will pay close attention to its story line in order to appreciate its "theology." That theology, moreover, is a bold assertion that the resurrection of Jesus is both "good news" for us who see it as God's promise of our own new life and also a confirmation of Jesus as the Son of God, the full expression of the Wisdom of God.

A. Composition and Structure

Underlying this approach are certain presuppositions which must be acknowledged. A nod of recognition and acceptance must be made first in the direction of that movement known as "form criticism" which over a half-century ago realized that the author of Mark was not an actual eyewitness of the events he reports but a compiler of the traditions about Jesus which Jesus' followers had preserved for several decades already before Mark gave them a permanent, written form. An immediate consequence of this now generally accepted intuition, of course, is that the indications of chronological sequence and geographical change of scene derive from the necessity of constructing a "framework" into which to place these units of traditional material and do not reflect much, if any, actual memory of how these traditions about Jesus corresponded to the history of Jesus himself. Events happen "before" and "after" each other because the evangelist has chosen to arrange the traditional materials in the order they now have in his gospel. When Mark smoothly joins one traditional unit of material to another, he is creating a "framework" in which the central figure of the gospel, Jesus, is seen to move from one setting and situation to the next. The result is an apparent biography, but the appearances result from Mark's own work as he moves largely free-floating, unspecified and disconnected traditional materials into an ordered, sequential narrative. Attention to this framework will, of course, help in the identification of the "plot line" of Mark's gospel.

An emphasis upon Mark as a compiler of traditions, however, must be balanced by an emphasis upon Mark as a true author. An attention to the techniques by means of which Mark edited the traditional materials and wove them together remains a mere exercise in analysis without a recognition also that the evangelist's work served a larger purpose: to convey through arrangement of the traditional materials and through editorial emphases in the framework material and in the traditions themselves a clear statement that was of considerable importance to him and to those who preserved the gospel of Mark as their own, handing it on to us. This second way of addressing the gospel has come to be known as "redaction criticism," and this book is guided by its insights.

Our approach will be (1) to recognize those characteristic ways in which Mark constructed a framework and arranged traditional materials; (2) to recognize the unity of thought thus accomplished in large portions of the gospel; (3) to arrive finally at a statement of that intention which guided the evangelist in his work. In doing so we attribute to Mark the full creativity accorded to any author, and in allowing his intention to come to expression, we realize the fundamental purpose of redaction criticism.

Determining the "full creativity" of Mark has been, of course, a notoriously difficult task for those who practice the methods of redaction criticism. It is possible to accumulate evidence for the modifications Matthew and Luke made when using as one of their sources the gospel of Mark: a careful comparison of those later gospels with their source yields positive results and, when they are consistent, a significant body of evidence. But with what can we compare the gospel of Mark so as to know, on a verifiable basis, what modifications Mark made in reporting the traditions which circulated before he wrote, since we have no copy of them in their pre-Markan form? The procedure followed here provides a term of comparison within the gospel itself: when a consistent theme is discoverable within the framework materials and in his overall arrangement of materials (steps 1 and 2 above), there is reason to suspect (although it cannot be further verified) that that theme is also due to the evangelist's creativity as an author when it appears within the traditional materials themselves.

Guided by these presuppositions, it would seem possible to identify both a large-scale structure for the gospel and the purpose it served. The structure which emerges is a concentric one, that is, a structure in which the parts of the whole move in order toward a mid-point and then, after the mid-point, reverse themselves so that there is a correspondence observable between the first and last parts, etc. Although this is not a way we organize literary works today, there is evidence that it was known and used in the first century. The advantage of this compositional technique is that it allows the plot line to progress, as it were, on a horizontal line from start to finish, from beginning to end, while at the same time "peaking" at the mid-point, establishing the point of emphasis, prepared for by what precedes the mid-point and developed by what follows it. The advantage for the evangelist Mark, in particular, was that it allowed him to portray an apparent historical sequence of events from Jesus' baptism to his death and resurrection while providing at the same time the insight with which to interpret those events at the middle section (8:27–10:45) where we learn the "first shall be last and the last, first" (10:31) and that he who was God's Son (9:7) must die in order to be raised from the dead (8:31; 9:31; 10:33).

The large-scale, concentric structure shown below is a new result which, not surprisingly, accords with a number of observations previously made about the gospel of Mark. Since no structure or plan for this gospel has won general approval before this, the arguments are set forth in separate chapters. There is interdependence here: if one section were fatally flawed in its argument, all would fall apart and the concentric structure would be irreparably damaged. Conversely, however, the probability of the weakest of the arguments for a section/part of the structure is enhanced by the strength of all the others.

Linking the significant parts of the gospel together are smaller passages like 1:16–20, 3:7–19, 6:14–29, 8:22–26, 10:46–52, 12:41–44, 14:1–10, and 15:40–47. These are episodes which illustrate model forms of discipleship and which should be seen as expressions of the emphasis the evangelist was making in the adjoining sections. They function both as narrative bridges joining one section to another and also as paradigms of discipleship.

What we propose is this:

A. Opening Section 1:1–15 Jesus is identified as Son of God
   1. interlude *1:16–20 Jesus' first followers*
  B. 1st Major Section 1:21–3:6 Jesus' ministry occasions opposition
    2. interlude *3:7–19 Of Jesus, disciples, mission*
   C. 2nd Major Section 3:20–6:13 Of response to Jesus, and judgment
     3. interlude *6:14–29 Baptist gives his life*
    D. 3rd Major Section 6:30–8:21 Jesus comes to Israel as its true teacher
      4. interlude *8:22–26 Healing of blind man*
     E. Central Section 8:27–10:45 The "secret" wisdom: giving all to all gains all, e.g. Jesus
      4' interlude *10:46–52 Healing of blind man*
    D' 3rd Last Section 11:1–12:40 Jesus comes to Israel as its Lord
     3' interlude *12:41–44 Widow gives all she has*
   C' 2nd Last Section 13:1–37 Of discipleship, judgment
    2' interlude *14:1–9 Of Jesus' departure and discipleship*
  B' Last Major Section 14:10–15:39 Betrayal, rejection and death of Jesus
   1' interlude *15:40–47 Jesus' last followers*
A' Climax 16:1–8 Jesus is confirmed as Son of God by his resurrection

The middle section is itself set in concentric form. The very middle of that section is the second resurrection prediction and an interpretation of it. Mark 8:27–10:45 overall is an interpretation of the death of Jesus in which it is not only seen as God's will for Jesus but, paradigmatically, God's will for all humankind. To be on the side of God (8:33) one must become the servant and slave of all (10:43–44), just as Jesus the Son of Man did (10:45). Indeed, from Mark 8:27–10:45 on, the reader is able to recognize that Jesus submits his will to that of the Father and does the things which must be done to accomplish that will, which is his own death; because of the references to the resurrection in 8:31, 9:9–10, 9:31 and 10:34 the reader also knows that vindication awaits Jesus for his acceptance of the cross and death and can anticipate that a similar vindication will await him if he pursues the same course (cf. 10:30). What is involved is nothing less than the acceptance of an submission to the events of history as an expression of the will of God; one's essential status is not the point. If Jesus, the Son of Man and Son of God, is the model, then he who is quintessentially the first is totally abased in order to be confirmed as first by the resurrection. The reader recognizes the unavoidability of the Father's will if one is to receive the Father's vindication and reads the balance of Mark's gospel with an understanding that prompts him to join in the centurion's exclamation of admiration, "Truly this man was (the) Son of God!" (15:39), even before the disciples themselves can make this confession in the gospel.

The structure of Mark's gospel, therefore, provides not only in its horizontal story-line the story of Jesus' life and death, but also in the central section of 8:27–10:45 a theological interpretation of what those events revealed for those to whom it is given to know the secrets of the kingdom of God (4:11).

B. The Wisdom Background of Mark

When Jesus finished telling the crowd the first of his parables, the one about the man who went out to sow seed (Mk 4:3–8), he cried out: "Let the man who has ears to hear, hear!" Jesus knew what we all come to learn— that there are times when what is required is a kind of "hearing" or insight or understanding which can perceive the meaning and intent behind mere words.

Often the meaning given to words is derived from the context in which they are heard. And in our time, the meaning we accord to the words of Mark's gospel is often derived from *our* context, and we "hear" those words as individuals well familiar with the Christian tradition's teaching about Jesus as the Son of God, the pre-existent second person in the Trinity. While that is *our* context, it was not necessarily the context which the author of the gospel of Mark anticipated for his audience. There is, for example, not a hint in Mark of the idea of Jesus as pre-existent, and we must always be careful not to insinuate into the minds and mouths and words of writers ideas which developed after them.

What is suggested in these pages is that the gospel of Mark can be understood clearly and well in terms of a context quite appropriate to the features of the gospel's text and of early Christianity's developing sense of the unique person who was Jesus. The context offered as the lens through which to view Mark's gospel is that of Jewish wisdom.

"Wisdom" is a word, too, whose meaning is not entirely certain at first hearing and about which we must say more shortly. Even "Jewish wisdom" is a multi-faceted phrase which applies to at least three different things: it is (1) an attitude toward the world which acknowledges experience of the world as a source of knowledge about how things ought to be, (2) a story or "myth" that legitimated that confidence in experiential knowledge, and (3) a collection of writings that came to express each of those two features. Because the gospel of Mark appears, as we shall see, to have been particularly influenced by one such writing (the Wisdom of Solomon), a bit more about these aspects of "Jewish wisdom" needs to be said.

1. From Experience to Knowledge to Wisdom

To speak of Jewish wisdom as an "attitude toward the world as a source of knowledge about how things ought to be" is to call attention to the effort of the sages of the ancient Near East to capture an element of truth in proverbial sayings. In the book of Proverbs, for example, one saying saw in the ant a lesson to be learned: "Go the ant, O sluggard; consider her ways and be wise. Without having any chief, officer or ruler, she prepares her food in summer, and gathers her sustenance in harvest" (Prov 6:6–8). Before that lesson can be drawn from the ways of the ant, however, there must already have been a perception of the truth of the lesson and a perception *also* that it can find apt expression in a lesson from the natural world. And so some truths can be expressed through comparisons drawn from the natural world:

> Like snow in summer or rain in harvest,
>   so honor is not fitting for a fool.
> Like a sparrow in its flitting,
>   like a swallow in its flying,
> a curse that is causeless does not alight"   (Prov 26:1–2).

But these comparisons only highlight the already perceived truth, as in the last phrasing of the comparison just given. Just as we might say today, "A stitch in time saves nine" or "An apple a day keeps the doctor away," so too the ancient sage could say "A man without self-control is like a city broken into and left without walls" (Prov 25:28) or "He who digs a pit will fall into it and a stone will come back upon him who starts it rolling" (Prov 26:27).

Proverbs and succinct expressions are presented, therefore, as truths which all must acknowledge because all must recognize that they correspond to the general experience of people everywhere. If sometimes they are strengthened by a comparison to the natural world, that only serves to indicate that they were drawn from an experience of that natural world in the first place. It is not, of course, the case that the proverbial expression is always and universally true: there will be some who will dig a pit and not fall into it and there will be some who will eat an apple a day and still get sick. But the power of these expressions is that they capture intuitively what *is* the *general* experience of humankind. That general experience, once given expression, is presented as truth and knowledge that those who would be "wise" must accept.

Yet this is only the first step, the beginning of a sophisticated and complex enterprise. For it is not a matter of one or two proverbs drawn from experience, but the accumulation of many such truths brought to expression, and it is in the amassing of such observations that the next question arises. Any collection of proverbial expressions must necessarily be incomplete because not all of human experience has been gathered and because human experience will continue to provide new materials for yet new proverbial expressions. And so the collection of these efforts to express the "truth" of things must be recognized as yet incomplete. Something more, some further insight is required, and those who would be truly "wise" must push beyond the proverb grounded in experience to a yet more profound comprehension, insight, understanding. The author of the book of Proverbs expresses his purpose thus:

> That the wise man also may hear and increase in learning,
>   and the man of understanding acquire skill,
> To understand a proverb and a figure,
>   the words of the wise and their riddles   (Prov 1:5–6).

This is no esoteric project. One needs wisdom and understanding in order to know how to live! What is good? What is evil? Even today an honest response to those questions will quickly bring us to the humbling awareness that, for all our scientific knowledge, we still cannot with sureness apply the ethical principles we have received from the generations which walked in our religious traditions before us. The division among

Christians in Northern and Southern Ireland, the warfare among Christians in Lebanon, the verbal (and sometimes not merely verbal) conflicts among American Christians over abortion, capital punishment, and national priorities are witness enough. Ours is an era proud of its scientific knowledge and its accomplishments, but the technology that made nuclear warfare possible cannot determine when and under what circumstances it might be "ethical" to use it; the technology that put televised images into most American homes cannot decide what kind of materials are "morally acceptable" to be shown on them. The kind of knowledge needed for us to decide between what is good and what is evil, to be a moral and ethical people, is simply of a different kind. One *still* needs wisdom and understanding in order to know how to live.

And so, many of the proverbial sayings are directed at how one should live:

> A slack hand causes poverty,
>> but the hand of the diligent makes rich   (Prov 10:4).
>
> He who walks in integrity walks securely,
>> but he who perverts his ways will be found out   (Prov 10:9).

And that concern for the ethical is obvious in the collection of these materials in the wisdom books of Judaism. Under the artifice of a father counseling his son, the author of Proverbs writes:

> Hear my son, and accept my words,
>> that the years of your life may be many.
> I have taught you the way of wisdom;
>> I have led you in the paths of uprightness. . . .
> Keep hold of instruction, do not let go;
>> guard her, for she is your life.
> Do not enter the path of the wicked,
>> and do not walk in the way of evil men   (Prov 4:10–11, 13–14).

In a somewhat simplistic way, accordingly, the world falls into two classes of people, the wise and the foolish (when one speaks of their understanding of the world); those two groups are virtually identical with the "righteous" and the "wicked," respectively (when one speaks of the kind of lives they lead). As that same context in Proverbs says:

But the path of the righteous is like the light of dawn,
   which shines brighter and brighter until full day.
The way of the wicked is like deep darkness;
   they do not know over what they stumble   (Prov 4:18–19).

Before going any further, it must be noticed that these two ways of being and living—the wise and righteous on the one hand, the foolish and wicked on the other—are understood as having a decisive outcome. The first is blessed in various ways, and the other is not. As Proverbs 11:19 says so succinctly, "He who is steadfast in righteousness will *live,* but he who pursues evil will *die.*" Not always is the contrasting fate stated in terms of such a final outcome; far more frequent is the assertion of "blessings" (Prov 10:6) of various kinds for the righteous and "calamity" (Prov 24:16) of various kinds for the wicked. Yet there is overall a sense of correspondence between wisdom or its rejection on the one hand and blessings or curses on the other. There is an association, therefore, between wisdom/righteousness, or its rejection, and one's ultimate fate.

That this should be so is not surprising among Jews who stood within a tradition where the fate of the entire people depended upon its keeping the covenant established with them by God; the giving of the commandments to Moses was set in the context of a promise of blessings if the commandments were kept and a threat of curses if they were not. Israel's concern was to be righteous before God. But, by extension, so too was it necessary for each Jew to be righteous before God, and to do that required knowing God's will for humankind even in those circumstances not obviously covered by the commandments and by the developed application of those commandments, the "ordinances" and "statutes" which the book of Deuteronomy so frequently mentions.

It was not the case that Jewish wisdom sought truth and ethical guidance only from experience and in isolation from the Jewish religious tradition. While there are parallels with the wisdom materials of other cultures and while there is much in the wisdom sayings that speaks to everyday matters (e.g. Prov 17:2), Jewish wisdom materials are set squarely within the religious tradition and are seen to supplement it. It was the *same* Lord God who had given the commandments who was also the source of "wisdom" (Prov 2:6) and who discerns the conduct of men and women (Prov 16:2, 11) and who actively intervenes to protect the righteous and to dismay the unrighteous (Prov 10:3). Indeed, it may have been that very need to know how to be righteous before God, a need established by God's covenant with the Jews, that stimulated and motivated the wisdom movement within Israel. Where the Mosaic commandments failed to be precise, where the traditional interpretations of them failed to be adequate or complete, precisely there could the wisdom movement turn to a different way of perceiving God's will for them, its experience of the world created by God.

The Jewish sage knew that his experience of the world was both the same as, and at the same time different from, the non-Jew's experience of the world. The physical and natural world was the same for both. But the Jew brought to it a special lens through which to view that experience; knowing that the God who had made the world was the same God who had made the covenant with Moses and the generations after him, the sage knew that a first and essential element was the "fear of the Lord," that acceptance of God as creator and as the source of all being and of the moral order as well. If observance of the Mosaic commandments could lead to a life that was at least an approximation of the moral order God willed for his people, it gave to the Jew an advantage in the quest for that which was the wisdom which penetrates all beings. To live in such a manner was to "fear" the Lord. The "fear of the Lord," then, was the starting point of all true wisdom.

The fear of the Lord is the beginning of knowledge;
fools despise wisdom and instruction   (Prov 1:7).

If the "fear of the Lord" could not always bring the Jew to a clear understanding of what God expected of men and women in certain situations, it could be supplemented by an experience of the world created by God. Here Jewish wisdom addresses the world with a different starting point from its neighbors' precisely because its quest for "knowledge" about the world is recognized as but a step toward an "understanding" of the world itself, of it as a whole. And that, in turn, it recognized as but the prerequisite for gaining the "wisdom" which was an understanding of God's plan for the men and women he had created. The purpose of the Mosaic covenant was to create a people holy unto God, righteous before him, one which lived by the righteousness of God himself. The purpose of the pursuit of "wisdom" was to find that very plan of God for humankind, the wisdom of God himself. Righteousness and Wisdom emanated from God, and each was the goal men and women sought to reach. Fundamentally, they were inseparable.

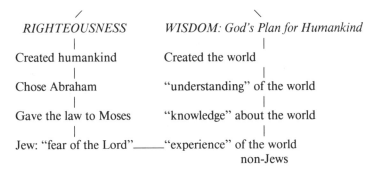

GOD

(Source of moral order and of being)

RIGHTEOUSNESS | WISDOM: *God's Plan for Humankind*

Created humankind | Created the world

Chose Abraham | "understanding" of the world

Gave the law to Moses | "knowledge" about the world

Jew: "fear of the Lord"——"experience" of the world
non-Jews

Hence the quest for "wisdom" was as religious as it was patently secular; for the Jewish sage, that modern distinction was not made. Knowledge gained through an experience of the world was knowledge about the world God had created, sustained and ruled over. It was the door through which one had access to the wisdom of God, to an understanding of God's plan for humankind, and as such it would amplify, but never really pervert, the holiness requirements of the law of Moses.

> Yes, if you cry out for insight
>   and raise your voice for understanding,
> If you seek it like silver
>   and search for it as for hidden treasures;
> *Then you will understand the fear of the Lord*
>   and find the knowledge of God.
> For the Lord gives wisdom . . .   (Prov 2:3–6).

2. Wisdom as Story

In a number of the Jewish "wisdom" writings there is a shift of focus to material in which wisdom is apparently personified. The shift of focus can be quite abrupt, as it is in Proverbs 1:19–21:

> Such are the ways of all who get gain by violence;
>   *it* takes away the life of its possessors.

> Wisdom cries aloud in the street;
>   in the markets *she* raises her voice;
> On the top of the walls she cries out;
>   at the entrance of the city gates she speaks . . .

And as the text continues, Wisdom (capitalized, in order to recognize the personification intended) addresses the "simple" (Prov 2:22); they have not heeded her call, have refused to listen, have not taken her outstretched hand (Prov 2:24–25), and so she announces their fate: when they call upon her, she will not answer nor respond (Prov 2:26–28). When did this refusal of Wisdom's call occur? It happened when "they hated knowledge," when they "did not choose the fear of the Lord" (Prov 2:29). As we noted above, there is here again that tight interconnection between the "fear of the Lord" and "wisdom" and one's fate. Indeed this passage ends with Wisdom's reassurance:

> He who listens to me will dwell secure
>   and will be at ease, without dread of evil   (Prov. 1:33).

In such a text is found only one thing really new: the presentation of the relationships described above in the form of a *story* about Wisdom. That which one is encouraged to seek out (Prov 2:2–4), which the Lord gives (Prov 2:6) in some manner through the "fear of the Lord" (Prov 2:5), has become a personage which gives of herself. Wisdom (personified) gives "wisdom," that understanding of God's plan for men and women which enables them to be righteous before God. That knowledge and "wisdom" which the sage had sought through an experience of the world so as to be "righteous" before God could not really be distinguishable from the plan which God had for creation and for humankind. The "wisdom" one sought was forever beyond one's grasp, for it was after all the wisdom of God. To personify the Wisdom of God is but to begin to put the relationships involved in the Jewish sage's approach to the world into the form of a story, but a story which begins on God's side of the world and before history, as it were. And, because the story began with God, it gives authority to and legitimates the truths which the Jewish sage drew from his experience of the created world and expressed in proverb and maxim.

How easily one could move from one focus to the other is seen not just in the absence of a transition between Proverbs 1:19 and 1:20; it is seen also in the change from speaking of "wisdom" as an "it" to a "her" (cf.

Prov 2:13–18). And it occurs as well in the ambiguity of Proverbs 3:19: "The Lord by wisdom founded the earth; by understanding he established the heavens," where "wisdom" can be an attribute of God like "understanding" *or* an independent being created by God and working with him in the creation of the world as Proverbs 8:22–31 portrays her.

It is impossible to identify the time and locality in which the speaking of Wisdom as though it were an independent entity began to draw to itself the elements of a story about Wisdom's history before the world existed and then of its presence among God's creatures; the "myth" about Wisdom, however, surely developed. Its presence in Israel perhaps derived from the use of an old Near Eastern myth, but in any event Israel employed these elements of a story about Wisdom in a manner thoroughly consistent with its religious perspective. Unfortunately, the Jewish story about Wisdom is known to us only in fragments of its features: Job 28, Proverbs 1 and 8, Sirach 1 and 24, Baruch 3, and Wisdom of Solomon 6–9 are important evidence that a story about Wisdom was a familiar one in Judaism, but motifs which are present in some texts may not be present in the others. While the most frequently recurring elements are Wisdom's concealment, her dwelling in heaven, her role in creation, her dwelling among those she has chosen, her call, her rejection by some and her choice of some, even in those texts where most of these elements are present, one or another may be missing: e.g. in Proverbs 1 and 8 the motif of concealment is missing, and in Sirach 1 and 24 there is probably no motif of rejection.

If one were to synthesize the elements of the Wisdom speculation from the fragments available to us, a coherent reconstruction would be the following:

Wisdom was created by God before God created the world.	Prov 8:22ff; Sir 1:4; 24:3, 5, 8b, 9
She was present at the creation of the world	Prov 8:27–30; Wis 9:9
and, indeed, was the agent through whom God created it.	Prov 3:19; 8:30; Wis 7:22
Her throne or dwelling place is appropriately beside God, in the heavens,	Job 28:12–27; Sir 1:1; 24:4; Wis 8:3f; 9:9f.
and her transcendence of and authority over the created world is complete.	Job 28:13–14; Sir 24:5; Wis 7:22f; 8:1

Hence Wisdom appears to created man as hidden, concealed.	Job 28:13f, 21f; Sir 1:6; 6:22; Wis 9:13–17
God accordingly sends Wisdom to man,	Prov 2:6; Sir 1:9f; 24:8a; Wis 9:10, 17
particularly to Israel,	Sir 24:8c, 10–14
where she teaches what is pleasing to God,	Sir 4:11, 18; Wis 7:21, 9:10
i.e. the "fear of the Lord"	Job 28:28; Prov 2:5; Sir 1:11–14, 16, 18, 20, 2:15
in the form of the "law."	Sir 2:16; 15:1; 24:23
Wisdom's presence is also an appeal to accept her.	Prov 1:20–23; 8:1–4; 9:3; Sir 24:19; Wis 6:13
Acceptance of her gives wisdom,	Prov 8:17; Sir 4:16
life,	Prov 3:16, 8:35; Sir 4:12
righteousness,	Prov 8:20; Wis 8:7
salvation,	Prov 1:33; 3:17; Sir 1:18–20; 4:13; Wis 6:19; 7:27; 8:13
wealth, etc.	Prov 8:18, 21; Sir 15:2–6; 24:15–17, 20–22; Wis 8:16ff
Hence, her value is incalculable.	Job 28:15–19; Prov 3:14f; 8:10f, 19.
Conversely, failure to accept her leads to her withdrawal of her gift (wisdom)	Prov 1:24–32; Sir 4:19; 6:6–8
and death.	Prov 8:36

The weight of textual instances concern the divine origin of Wisdom, her accessibility through the Jewish law and the blessings and curses which are heaped upon the acceptance or rejection of Wisdom by Wisdom herself. It may well be that the story developed differently within Judaism, emphasizing in some contexts the identification with the Mosaic law as the vehicle for achieving the righteousness expected by God on the one hand or in other contexts stressing a companionship of the wise with Wisdom and, through her, with God.

The "story" about Wisdom may be legitimately called a "myth," if one understands that term correctly as the effort to express through the texture and imagery of a story what can never be adequately stated directly, a truth or truths that are not empirical but are perceived to be of ultimate importance. For us to take the "story" about Wisdom in some hardened form would be to miss the relationships between the sage, the world and God which the story authenticates. Yet it cannot be ignored, either, that this story, once it had taken its place among the traditions of Israel, was available for appropriation as a category of interpretation for telling the story of Jesus. Moreover, two directions of emphasis could be taken, one stressing an association of Wisdom with the law of Moses and the other stressing the companionship with God accessible through the possession of "wisdom."

3. *Wisdom Literature and the Wisdom of Solomon*

We have already referred to some texts in which the story of Wisdom appears. What this section presents is not more about those particular texts but a brief description of what is called "wisdom literature."

When the sage generated his intuitive insights about God's plan for men and women from his own experience of the created world, that was the beginning of a larger enterprise, the effort to teach others to look upon the world in a similar fashion. Whenever the wisdom perspective found expression in written form, we find "wisdom literature." Sometimes it is embedded in a work of an entirely different kind, as, for example, Psalms 1 and 37. Sometimes it is the controlling feature of entire books like Proverbs, Ecclesiastes, Sirach and the Wisdom of Solomon. All these materials are part of the "wisdom literature" of Israel.

Besides the story about Wisdom, there is another aspect of the wisdom literature which is pertinent for our reading of the gospel of Mark, a concern about the apparent inequity of God's dealing with his faithful. On the one hand, there was the conviction that if one observed God's commandments and was righteous under the law, one would be "blessed" by God; and he who did not live by this "fear of the Lord" would be weighted down with all manner of calamities. Yet experience did not always bear out this conviction, and the sage, whose confidence in his experience of the world would not turn away from the inconsistency, dealt with it. The book of Job is a beginning effort to reconcile the traditional teaching with the fact of experience, and its answer is that one cannot reduce the wisdom of God to a simple quid-pro-quo formula.

But that is not an entirely satisfactory answer, particularly when it is challenged by the harsh reality of death. Some die unrewarded, others die unpunished; some were blessed, others were not. Since death was a barrier beyond which one could not go, it prompted "the Preacher" (Ecclesiastes) to pronounce everything "vanity," since nothing lasted but for its own time and then it ceased to be; even the seeking after "wisdom" is an "unhappy business" (Eccl 1:13).

> For the fate of the sons of men and the fate of beasts is the same; as one dies, so dies the other. They all have the same breath, and man has no advantage over the beasts; for all is vanity. All go to one place; all are from the dust, and all turn to dust again. Who knows whether the spirit of man goes upward and spirit of the beast goes down to the earth? (Eccl 3:19–21).

Death, then, challenged the traditional conviction that God's covenant kindness brought "blessings" of a real and substantial kind. Despite the final urging of the Preacher, "Fear God, and keep all his commandments; for this is the whole duty of man" (Eccl 12:13), the question had been raised: just what is the fate of the righteous and the unrighteous if death is the end of all our being?

It is to this question that the Wisdom of Solomon asserts a new answer: the righteous will have a continuance beyond death! Even if at the time of their death they have not yet received the blessings which are their reward for living according to God's will, death is not the end for them and their righteousness will not go unrewarded. Death has its origin, after all, not with God but with the ungodly (Wis 1:13, 16; 2:23f), and the "souls of the righteous are in the hand of God" (Wis 3:1); it may seem that they have died, but "they are at peace" (Wis 3:3) and "their hope is full of immortality" (Wis 3:4). That affirmation of immortality for the righteous is made through the paradigmatic story of the conspiracy of the "ungodly" against the "righteous man" in Wisdom 1:16–5:14. The words of the ungodly in Wisdom 2:1–11 summarize the pessimistic teaching of the Preacher aptly, and the entire narrative in Wisdom 2–5 is really the response to that pessimistic view of death. A clear affirmation of the continuance of the righteous beyond death is resoundingly expressed in Wisdom 5:15f:

> But the righteous live for ever,
>   and their reward is with the Lord;
>   the Most High takes care of them.
> Therefore they will receive a glorious crown
>   and a beautiful diadem from the hand of the Lord,
> Because with his right hand he will cover them,
>   and with his arm he will shield them.

It is here in this affirmation that the Jewish Wisdom tradition had moved to a truth which could not be drawn from its experience of the world; the Preacher was more correct in that regard. But the interaction between the religious experience of Israel and the empirical experience of the world had been reversed. If "experience of the world" could not supplement the religious teaching of Israel about the way in which God would keep his covenant promises, as the Preacher so clearly saw, then the religious teaching of Israel must supplement the experience of the world and defy the finality even of death in order to preserve faith and confidence in God's covenant with the righteous.

4. *From Wisdom to the Gospel of Mark*

We noted before that often how we understand a saying or a text depends upon our context, where we stand when we attend to it. What we have but sketched here is a way of being Jewish which was thoroughly religious, grounding all being and all wisdom in the one God Israel worshiped, while also addressing the world of experience as having positive value. To be "righteous" before God was of paramount importance, but that task required the pursuit of, the knowledge of, the understanding of God's plan for humankind. The search for "wisdom" was at the same time a response to God's own appeal to men and women, an appeal uttered by "Wisdom." Sometimes that appeal came to the Jew through the law of Moses; sometimes it came through the disclosure of God's creative imprint on the world as glimpsed through man's experience of it.

The wisdom way of being Jewish had come to challenge even the finality of death in the Wisdom of Solomon, a writing that was very influential among Hellenistic Jews (it was written in Greek) not too long before the gospel of Mark was written. In the Wisdom of Solomon the "righteous man" is described in a way that seems to be appropriate also as a description for Jesus in the gospel of Mark. Particularly striking is the detail that he "boasts that God is his father" (Wis 2:16) so that the ungodly determine "to test what will happen at the end of his life" (Wis 2:17), to see "if the righteous man is God's son" (Wis 2:18). The gospel of Mark develops the concerns of the Jewish wisdom tradition in a number of ways, as we shall see; and the Appendix shows the parallels which can be made between the story told about Wisdom and the righteous man in whom she presences herself (Wis 7:27) on the one hand, and Mark's gospel about Jesus on the other hand. But there is one specific way in which the gospel of Mark adds to what had preceded it: where the Wisdom of Solomon could only affirm from its religious faith that "the righteous live for ever," the gospel of Mark can proclaim the "good news!" that in Jesus' resurrection we have *experience and confirmation* of the immortality of the righteous (this emphasis on the resurrection of Jesus is further described on pages 152–154). It is indeed "good news!" which the gospel of Mark proclaims (Mk 1:1).

A. Mark's Opening Section 1:1–15

Jesus Is Identified as Son of God

It is in the very opening lines of a work that an author suggests to his reader the theme or themes that will be developed; here is where it is necessary to ignite interest in and recognition of the importance of the work's focus. And Mark is no less clever an author than any other: he presents in his opening fifteen verses a self-contained unit that at the beginning and the end focuses upon the two fundamental themes of his work: Jesus as the Son of God and the "good news" by which Jesus brought about the kingdom of God.

Some might think that the gospel of Mark starts abruptly because its first verse is often translated "The beginning of the gospel of Jesus Christ, the Son of God." The very first verse seems heavy and self-important as it seems to say, in effect, "Here begins the book" about Jesus. Yet that sense of Mark's beginning comes from understanding "gospel" as referring to the written gospel of Mark itself, an interpretation that comes easily to us who are so familiar with the "four gospels" of Matthew, Mark, Luke and John, the first four books of the New Testament. Yet when Mark wrote there were no written gospels, and that interpretation was not possible. Mark's readers knew that "gospel" meant the "good news." An appropriate paraphrase of Mark's first verse would be "This is where the 'good news' that is the story of Jesus, the Son of God, begins."

Whether the "beginning" of that good news was intended to refer only to the preliminaries of Mark's first fifteen verses or to everything he wrote about Jesus can perhaps never be finally decided. What is clear, however, is that this exciting, important "good news" concerned Jesus Christ, the Son of God. One possible way of stating that is to say it was the "good news brought by Jesus the Son of God." (Even in English the ambiguity in the "gospel of Jesus Christ" is clear; is it the gospel about Jesus or the gospel which Jesus possesses?) What suggests that Mark's sense of the phrase was that Jesus brought the "good news" is the scene in 1:14–15 where Jesus does, in fact, preach the "good news" and call men to "Repent! And believe in the good news!"

It is not yet clear, of course, what the content of that "good news" is which men should believe and embrace. Mark here only announces the beginning of the story; the story which Mark tells in the rest of his account will then make it clear what that content is.

If 1:1 is understood as the approximate equivalent to a "title," either of this opening section of the gospel or of the entire gospel (to 16:8) or both, then the verses which follow present four scenes moving directly toward their climax in 1:14–15 and Jesus' proclamation of the "good news," and the four scenes really comprise two units, the first introducing the Baptist, giving him authority and citing his words, and the second introducing Jesus, giving him authority and citing his words; it is Jesus' words "believe in the good news!" which are in the position of climax. And the whole unit 1:1–15 is tightly compressed into one piece by the repetition in 1:15 of the phrase "good news" from 1:1.

1:1	"The beginning of the good news of Jesus Christ, the Son of God"
1:2–3	Scriptural authorization for the Baptist,
4–6	and popular acknowledgement of him
1:7–8	John's preaching, about Jesus
1:9–11	Direct, divine authorization for Jesus
12–13	and demonic and angelic acknowledgement of him
1:14–15	Jesus' preaching of the gospel, about the kingdom

First a citation of Isaiah speaks of the "messenger" who prepares the way of the Lord in vss. 2–3. When John the Baptist is introduced in vs. 4 by the narrator, the two figures are associated: John is the messenger who prepares the way. The narrator tells the reader three things about the Baptist: (1) he preached "a baptism of repentance"; (2) he was enormously popular as "all the country of Judea . . . and all the people of Jerusalem" responded to him; (3) he was in his appearance clearly a prophetic figure.

The figure of the Baptist has been given authority by the citation of the text from Isaiah; the continuity with the prophetic hope that was Israel's heritage is explicit and importance is given, for those who ascribe to that hope, to the words of the Baptist which follow. The phrase in 1:7, "and he proclaimed publicly," gives the messenger's testimony that the one to come "after me" will be far "more powerful" than his messenger and will come with a Holy Spirit.

John the Baptist may be viewed as one of God's mightiest prophets, anticipated even in the words of Isaiah as part of God's plan, but he himself looks ahead to the one who comes after him and in whose presence the Baptist thinks of himself as completely unworthy. The focus and interest has shifted with these words to this new figure, whom Isaiah called "the Lord" and whom the Baptist announces will "baptize" with "the Holy Spirit." If scripture authorizes the testimony of the Baptist, that testimony in turn announces the coming of one who will be "Lord" and who will bring the Spirit.

Mark swiftly and clearly identifies who this figure is. Two "scenes," vss. 9–13 and vss. 14–15, develop this enigmatic announcement of God's plan by the Baptist.

In 1:9–13 Jesus comes into John's orbit and is baptized by him. There are two "immediate" consequences to this act of obedience when Jesus submits to John's baptism "of repentance for the forgiveness of sins" (1:4): the Spirit descends upon Jesus and a voice from heaven announces: "*You* are my beloved Son; with you I am well pleased." The words of the voice from heaven in 1:11 are in the second person, directly addressed to Jesus; there is nothing to imply that anyone else was privy to them or knew that Jesus was now the Spirit-graced Son of God—except, of course, the *reader* of (or listener to) Mark's account. That Mark did not mean to suggest that others heard the words of the voice from heaven is the only plausible explanation of the bafflement and amazement which met Jesus everywhere during his ministry, as it is described in Mark's gospel. *To the reader,* Jesus is, as vs. 1 had announced, indeed the Son of God, attested to by God himself. And in the presence of the Baptist, the Baptist's own testimony, unknown to him, has been realized because Jesus, as God's Son, bearing the Spirit, has come, far "more powerful" and more "worthy" than even the Baptist.

It is appropriate to observe that Mark thought of his audience as having an allegiance to Israel's heritage; the citation from Isaiah shows that clearly. It is appropriate also to observe that the designation of the perfectly righteous one as a "son of God" had been made in the Wisdom of Solomon 2:18; to someone familiar with that work, it is God who gives Wisdom (Wisdom 7:7; 8:21; 9:6, 10), and the Wisdom of God is a "holy" "Spirit" (Wisdom 7:22) and the scene in Mark 1:9–11 would be the dramatic realization of the principle expressed in Wisdom 7:27: "in every generation she [Wisdom] passes into holy souls and makes them friends of God, and prophets." Mark not only links his account of Jesus to Israel's prophetic hope but he also situates it squarely in Israel's wisdom tradition and its hope for God's blessing of immortality upon the righteous.

Mark does not suggest that what follows happens later and was a separate incident (as do Matthew 4:1 and Luke 4:1). Rather the narrative continues directly along: the Spirit of vs. 10 "immediately" drives Jesus out into "the wilderness," where he is tempted by Satan and ministered to by angels (1:12–13). In the three phrasings of 1:13 the reader recognizes that this Jesus of Nazareth, baptized by John in the Jordan, acts no longer in a purely historical context. A contest of wills and allegiances is joined into with Satan: Jesus has shown his radical obedience to the will of the Father by responding to the call of the Baptist; the Father then approves that obedience by naming Jesus his Son; and when Satan "tempts" Jesus it can only be an effort to divert Jesus from that radical obedience. Mark only suggests the protection of God for Jesus, his Son, during this "testing" experience in reporting that "the angels ministered to him." If God has proclaimed Jesus to be his beloved Son, and he comes with the Spirit (1:10) and is led ("driven") by the Spirit, to be tempted by Satan, an eschatological, end-of-historical-time drama is taking shape. And all this Mark accomplishes with the simplest of phrasings in 1:12–13!

Yet one other link with the Wisdom of Solomon is suggested here. The righteous one in Wisdom is tested also (Wis 2:17) by those who belong to the party of the devil (2:24). And there as here in Mark 1:13, he is protected (Wis 3:1–5). This compilation of motifs echoing those of the early chapters of the Wisdom of Solomon suggest an effort by Mark to say to his audience: in this story about Jesus the immortality we hope for will be made real for us.

This opening section of the gospel draws to a close in 1:14–15. In vs. 14 Mark not so subtly identifies Jesus as the one about whom the Baptist had preached: Jesus comes "*after* John was arrested," just as the Baptist had said he would come "after" him (1:7). The Spirit-graced eschatological figure comes and proclaims the "good news *of God*," that "the present age has reached its end and the kingdom of God has come near." Here the reader learns in a most summary way to what the "good news" of 1:1 had alluded: a new reality has been brought to men by Jesus. Men need only change their lives, "repent," and embrace this "good news."

Mark 1:1–15 stands as a coherent whole, therefore, as it sketches the "beginning" of the drama in which "the present age has reached its end and the kingdom of God has come near." In Jesus' proclamation of the fulfillment of time and the appearance of the kingdom of God, a challenge has been made to men. Who will respond, what will the response require, and how will the story continue?

1. The First Interlude 1:16–20

Jesus' First Followers

Mark had surely expected his reader to recognize that Jesus' ringing proclamation of the "good news of God" ended the introductory phase of his story in which Jesus is identified as its central figure, the Spirit-graced Son of God. The narrative now turns to the response to Jesus' proclamation: first described is the immediate and total acceptance of Jesus' call by the four who will be the "inner core" of Jesus' disciples (1:16–20); then it will be clear that not all responded so quickly or with such full commitment, as we shall see (1:21–3:6).

Here Mark provides the reader with the first of the transitional episodes which link sections of the gospel together. What is characteristic of all of them is that they offer paradigms or models of discipleship, and none does so more clearly than this one. In the episode narrated in 1:16–20, two smaller scenes of virtually identical structure are presented: Jesus goes along the sea, sees two men, calls them, and immediately they leave what they are doing and "follow" him. In the first scene, Simon/Peter and Andrew are called to become "fishers of men"; in the second scene, James and John, the sons of Zebedee, are called, presumably to the same mission. Here it is clear that discipleship entails not only an immediate acceptance of and response to Jesus' call, but also a movement to extend that call of Jesus to yet others, to become "fishers of men."

The episode opens with Jesus going to the place where Peter and Andrew were working as fishermen; his first public address to individuals in this gospel is to these two men and his appeal is simple: "Come with me." This is really addressed as much to the reader as it is to Peter and Andrew, for from this point forward the reader will be confronted with the necessity of deciding where to place his or her allegiance. Jesus' words are a simple appeal to place that allegiance with him.

It is hard to miss Mark's emphasis here. Each of the two scenes (1:16–18; 1:19–20) ends with the identical phrasing, "they followed him." Jesus calls men and women to turn away from whatever it is they are doing and to be "with him" and to seek out others to do the same. The challenge is to accept that appeal and to accept it "immediately" and promptly, as Peter and Andrew did, to become disciples who "follow" Jesus.

In this first transitional episode setting forth an image of perfect discipleship, Mark also draws upon motifs from the Jewish tradition about Wisdom. Just as Jesus is seen going to the Sea of Galilee where Peter and Andrew and James and John are going about their usual occupation, so too Wisdom, it is said, "goes about seeking those worthy of her, and she graciously appears to them in their paths" (Wis 6:16; cf. 6:13). That appeal of Wisdom to men is also prominent in Proverbs 1:20–21, 8:1–5, and 9:3–6, and in that last text it is clear that what Wisdom offers is fellowship with herself, under the image of eating her bread and drinking her wine at her table in her house, an appeal in essence to be "with her" (cf. Wis 8:16–18), just as Jesus' appeal is to be "with him" (1:17). And it is Wisdom's task to "save" humankind by teaching them what is pleasing to God (Wis 9:18; cf. 9:9), and to this purpose she enlists others to help her; those who become her associates she in turn sends out to call others (Prov 9:3), a motif parallel to Jesus' call of his first disciples to become "fishers of men."

These motifs are yet further elaboration of the association of Jesus with Wisdom in the baptism narrative (1:10–11). If the Spirit which descended upon Jesus at the baptism is understood as Wisdom who is a Holy Spirit (Wis 7:22), who enters into the souls of the righteous, making them friends of God (Wis 7:27), then Wisdom has been shown to have presenced herself in Jesus, and Jesus, in turn, has taken up Wisdom's mission, to call men and women to himself and to save them by teaching what is pleasing to God. This story of Jesus has accordingly taken on soteriological implications at its very beginning. And the reader of Mark's account has been challenged by this appeal of Jesus to be with him because it is Wisdom's own appeal, offering life to those who accept it.

B. Mark's First Major Section 1:21–3:6

Jesus' Ministry Occasions Opposition

As Mark continues his recounting of the "good news!" it becomes clear how the first of the questions implicit in Jesus' proclamation of the kingdom of God will be answered. The response will be diverse. The reader, of course, is aware of the importance of the drama which is unfolding because Mark has made the reader a witness of the baptism scene and of the testimony of God to Jesus; and if that reader were also familiar with the Jewish wisdom motifs which came to expression there, he or she could only have had a more intense appreciation of the life and death consequences Jesus' ministry would have. That awareness in this first major section of Mark's narrative seems to be shared only by the demonic world which recognizes Jesus' appearance as the coming of the "Holy One of God" (1:24) to "destroy" it. The reaction of Jesus' human contemporaries is diverse: while the apostles "follow" Jesus, the crowds are uncomprehending and "astounded," although enthusiastic, and the religious authorities significantly begin to plot against him.

Mark shows those reactions as separate and sequential. After the episode by the Sea of Galilee where Jesus calls the first apostles, the next scene, to which we now turn, shows wider response at Capernaum. Then Mark pictures Jesus going throughout all the towns of Galilee and being enormously popular. The following scene then returns to the locale of Capernaum and describes developing opposition.

The response to Jesus' coming, therefore, is massive and widespread, if still uncomprehending of who Jesus is, and of what, therefore, the kingdom of God requires of men. But the storm clouds of opposition gather, intimating that the story will not be one with a humanly happy ending.

Now that Mark has associated the four principal disciples, Peter and Andrew, James and John, with Jesus, he moves Jesus into his first public appearance, a full and busy day of activity in Capernaum, 1:21–34.

In this sketch of the opening of Jesus' public ministry two things are emphatically demonstrated: Jesus comes with an authority that amazes (1:22) and astounds (1:27) and also with a control over the demonic world that is absolute. Jesus' control over the demonic is evident from the start, both in his casting out of the unclean spirit and in his commanding it to silence (1:23–25), motifs which are repeated only a few verses later (1:34). The demons "know" (1:24, 34) that Jesus comes as the Spirit-graced Son of God; so, too, does the reader of the gospel; but as is apparent from the response of astonishment and amazement, no one else does. This "secrecy motif" serves two purposes: it underscores the authority and power of Jesus' *word,* for it is with only his word that Jesus overcomes the power of the demonic; and, secondly, it keeps Jesus' being the Son of God (here: the "Holy One of God") from being publicly known. Until Jesus has been obedient to the Father in his death on the cross, he cannot be publicly known as the Son of God, which is what the resurrection event attests, as Mark 9:9 will indicate. The intimation of that other Markan emphasis, the reality of Jesus' resurrection, is subtle but certainly present in these silencings of the demons, "because they knew who he was" (1:34).

The materials in 1:21–34 have been given an elaborate framework by Mark. There are really three separate and distinct reports here—the report that Jesus taught with authority (1:22), the report that Jesus cast out an "unclean spirit" (1:23b–26), and the healing of Simon's mother-in-law —which have been tightly combined and elaborated by Mark. In order to move Jesus and the disciples from "the sea" into a setting appropriate for Jesus to be teaching, Mark pens the transitional phrasing in 1:21. Because Mark wants to combine the motif of authority with that of Jesus' control over demons, the transitional phrasing at the beginning of 1:23 is minimal. Mark reveals his true interest in 1:27 which combines the two motifs ("And everyone was astounded, so that they asked one another: 'What's this? A new teaching, given with authority! And he gives order to the unclean spirits, and they obey him'"). Mark 1:27 could only have been written by the individual who had brought the traditions in 1:22 and 1:23b–26 together. That authority over the demonic, Mark asserts, was responded to with complete "astonishment," with the result that his "fame spread everywhere" (1:28).

Mark has one more vignette to illustrate the complete authority of Jesus, the healing of Simon's mother-in-law. Verse 29 is Mark's transitional phrasing, and he indicates that the reader should view this miracle story as intrinsically connected to the synagogue episode: it happens "immediately" afterward. The story itself is not elaborated (indeed, the frequent repetition of "and" may indicate that an abbreviation of a once longer story has been made), but it does serve to show that this authoritative figure, Jesus, has power also over sickness and disease—the curse imposed upon Adam's descendants is no longer powerful, another sign that a radically new "beginning" is taking place.

In sketching these emphases of the authoritative teaching of Jesus and of his control over the unclean spirits, Mark is reminding his reader again of the characteristics of Wisdom as they are sketched in the Wisdom of Solomon 7:22–25 and now made present to men in Jesus:

> *Wisdom*, the fashioner of all things, *taught* me. For in her there is a *spirit* that is intelligent, *holy*, unique, manifold, subtle, mobile, clear, unpolluted, distinct, invulnerable, loving the good, keen, irresistible, beneficent, humane, steadfast, sure, free from anxiety, *all-powerful*, overseeing all, and penetrating through all spirits that are intelligent and pure and most subtle . . . for she is *a breath of the power of God* . . . therefore nothing defiled gains entrance into her.

Then, in an expansion of these episodes, 1:32–34 brings this first day of Jesus' public ministry to a close (note vs. 32a: "that evening, at sundown") by generalizing that "they brought to him all who were sick (like Simon's mother-in-law) or possessed with demons (like the man in the synagogue) . . . and he healed many who were sick and cast out many demons; and he would not permit the demons to speak, because they knew him." Mark, with these summarizing verses, has given the reader a sense of what characterizes the public appearance of Jesus as he brings into reality the kingdom of God: the absolute authority of Jesus over the demonic world and over the defects of humankind which result from sin. Jesus, then, comes as the preacher of the kingdom (1:14–15), the teacher of what men must do to enter it (1:22), although this has not yet been illustrated, the

Holy One with control over the demonic world and the healer of men. Since these all combine in Jesus, they are but variants of the one theme: with Jesus' coming, God is bringing his kingdom to men. As variants of a single theme, these characteristics of Jesus' activity are, if mentioned singly, nonetheless suggestive of the others, as Mark immediately shows.

In the central scenes of this section, 1:35–39, 40–45, Mark sharpens this picture. The evangelist provides an extensive transition in order to express Jesus' program of action: in vs. 35, Jesus on the morning of the second day of his public activity withdraws to "a desolate place" to pray; in vss. 36–37a Mark shows that the disciples who have been "with him" in the previous episodes *follow* him now and ask him to return to Capernaum and continue his work there. Jesus' response in vs. 38 is programmatic: "I have come out" to "preach" in the next towns also. And vs. 39 shows Jesus doing just that: throughout Galilee he "preaches" in the synagogues and "casts out demons," two activities which bring the kingdom of God into reality now "throughout all Galilee." Here, again, the story of Jesus as Mark tells it is reminiscent of the story told of Wisdom in the Jewish tradition: Wisdom calls out to men:

> Does not wisdom call,
> does not understanding raise her voice?
> On the heights beside the way,
> in the paths she takes her stand;
> besides the gates in front of the town,
> at the entrance of the portals she cries aloud:
> "To you, O men, I call . . ." (Prov 8:1–4).

The motif of Proverbs 8 was anticipated in Proverbs 1:20–22; and it is echoed in the Wisdom of Solomon 6:13–14:

> She hastens to make herself known to those who desire her.
> He who rises *early* to seek her will have no difficulty,
> for he will find her sitting at his gates.

The healing of a leper reported in 1:40–44 supplies an important and missing element, for it not only demonstrates the essential compassion of Jesus but it also subordinates the Jewish laws of purification to that compassion. The episode is joined tightly to the preceding verses by the simplest indication of succession, "and." In touching the "unclean" leper

(1:41) Jesus indicates the end of the power of the laws of purification by means of which Jews had sought to be "clean" or righteous before God. In healing the leper with the simple word, "Be clean" (1:41), Jesus not only provides evidence of his authority but suggests again that with his coming there is another beginning for humankind; little, after all, separates the authoritative word of Jesus, "Be clean," from the authoritative word of God at creation, "Let there be light." It should not be ignored that Mark includes in this story that the leper should present himself to the priest "for a proof to the people" (1:44); this healing is to become part of Jesus' public proclamation that "the kingdom of God is at hand."

Finally, in vs. 45 Mark draws this programmatic summary of Jesus' activity to a close by observing that the response to Jesus became so extensive "that it was no longer possible for Jesus to go openly into a town" (his intention in vs. 38!) but must rather remain "out in the deserted places" where people can come to him "from all directions." Thus the picture is clear: Jesus' bringing of the kingdom of God (as preacher, teacher, Holy One and healer) met with ever-increasing, if uncomprehending, popular response.

Mark turns to the closing scenes in this section, 2:1–3:6, by having Jesus return to the particular town where his public activity had begun (cf. 1:21), Capernaum; the transitional verses in 2:1–2 continue the theme of popular response: so many gather to hear his preaching that "not even the space in front of the door could any longer hold them." Against this setting and in the larger context of the massive popular response in 1:21–45, the next series of episodes portrays a *different* response, a growing opposition by a few, who are pointedly representatives of *religious* groups.

In the first episode (2:3–12), the healing of the paralytic is shown for what it is, a sign that the curse of sin is yielding to the power of the kingdom of God. The first group to challenge Jesus recognizes precisely that what Jesus is doing requires the power of God; but whereas the people reacted with wonder and were "astounded" when Jesus first opened his ministry in Capernaum, this group of scribes reacts with immediate rejection and indicts Jesus of "blasphemy! Who can forgive sins but the one God?" What Mark has been careful to portray and emphasize from 1:21 to this point is the "authority" of Jesus, and Jesus recognizes this response of the scribes for what it is, a challenge to the power and authority he bears (2:10). The miracle story is not recounted with an interest in reporting what happened so much as to illustrate the authority, once again, which Jesus has over disease and sin and to turn aside this challenge to that authority. Once again the crowd is "astonished" and, *unlike* the scribes, glorified God. It is also not to be ignored that Mark summarizes the crowd's astonishment with the phrase, "Never have we seen the like of this!" Yet again the radical newness of what was "beginning" (1:1) with Jesus is underscored.

The episode with the scribes is the first of several instances of opposition to Jesus. In order to include the next one, where Jesus sits at table with tax collectors and sinners (2:15–17), Mark has Jesus first call Levi to be a disciple. In many respects this call of Levi matches the call of the first four disciples in 1:16–20: Jesus is "beside the sea"; he utters the simple call "Follow me"; and it is noted that Levi "followed him." Apart from the traditional memory that Levi was the son of Alphaeus and a tax collector, therefore, 2:13–14 is probably best seen as part of the Markan framework, easing the narrative into the next episode.

In 2:15–18 several themes of the previous episode (2:1–12) reappear. There is opposition to Jesus' associating with those who are "unclean" under the Jewish laws of purity, the "sinners." The opposition comes from representatives of a religious group, i.e. from the "scribes of the Pharisees," who with their "Why...?" question again show a lack of comprehension of Jesus' mission and extend a challenge to it. And Jesus, in response, explicitly announces that he "came" (compare 1:38) to call "sinners." Mark in this section of his gospel describes Jesus' extending in particular ways the general proclamation of 1:14–15 that "the kingdom of God is at hand." And in the various parts of that description, it becomes clear that the "good news" is that God is bringing to men immersed in sin and its consequences (demonic control and disease) a hope for a new start.

The insistence that men stand now in the presence of a radically new overture of God toward men is continued in the next episode where the "Why...?" question (2:18), this time by disciples both of the Baptist and of the Pharisees, is prelude to three images of newness: a wedding (2:19–20), a patch on an old garment (2:21), and new wine (2:22). In each case the contrast is between the old and the new, climaxing in the third image: "No one pours new wine into old wineskins ... new wine is poured into new wineskins!" The old historical order stood under the curse of sin ever since Adam's disobedience in the garden of Eden; but now "the time is fulfilled" (1:15) and that historical order stands in the presence of the kingdom of God brought by Jesus. The two are as incompatible as new wine in old wineskins. Jesus' coming is a call to sinners (2:17) to "repent and believe in the good news" (1:15).

The fourth episode (2:23–28) in this series involves yet another "Why. . . ?" question (2:23), this time about Jesus' disciples not observing the sabbath. The challenge comes this time from the Pharisees themselves. Mark provides two responses to the sabbath issue: both from precedents in scripture. In the first response (2:25–26) Jesus argues from a precedent established by David in which the laws of ritual purification were subordinated to the needs of the starving. And in the second, Jesus draws the logical conclusion from the sequence of events in Genesis 1; humankind was created on the sixth day, *before* the sabbath, so that it could be said "the sabbath came into being for the sake of the man, and not the man for the sake of the sabbath; but if that is the case, then the descendants of those first human beings (collectively, "the *son* of the man," Adam) remain more important than the sabbath observance even now. Sabbath observance was, like other purity laws, an aid to becoming righteous in an historical order struggling under the curse of sin and its consequences. With Jesus' coming and the advent of the kingdom of God, sabbath observance has no power because God has chosen a radically new way to draw men and women to righteousness and its reward.

When Mark turns to the final episode (3:1–5) in this series, he places it "again" in "the synagogue." When Jesus had opened his public activity in 1:21, it was in the synagogue; there, too, as here it was "on the sabbath" (1:21; 3:1); and there, too, as here it was the setting for a miracle. If that first appearance of Jesus had demonstrated his authority and led to the astonishment of all, this time "*they* watched him to see whether he would heal him on the sabbath, *so that they could denounce him*" (3:2). Because of the unity of 2:1–3:6, the "they" in context can only be a general allusion to the religious leadership of the Jews instanced in the preceding four episodes; that narrow reference is confirmed in 3:6 with the naming of the Pharisees as taking the initiative. The opposition to Jesus is now real and fixed. Jesus meets it head-on by making of the situation a challenge to his opponents (vs. 4), and he is moved to anger at their silence and refusal to speak to a dilemma posed by the sabbath observance: "Is it lawful on the sabbath to do a good deed or to do evil, to save a life or to kill?" (vs. 4). The restoration of the man's hand gives *Jesus'* answer and is, at the same time, a counter-challenge to his religious opponents. They do not ignore it but "immediately formed a plan . . . against him in order that they might destroy him" (3:6). Mark has now warned his reader that Jesus' proclamation of the kingdom, despite its character as the realization of a new overture of God toward humankind and its prompting many to respond and "follow him" and "glorify God," occasioned also an opposition that could lead to his death. The description of the triumph of Jesus' opponents and of Jesus' death Mark will give in 14:10–15:39 where "the death of Jesus" is narrated, the section at the end of the gospel which corresponds to this one in the concentric structure.

Yet again the elements of the drama in the Wisdom of Solomon are echoed here in the hostile reaction of the religious leaders toward Jesus. Their watching Jesus closely so as to be able to denounce him (3:2) is not unlike the attitude of the "ungodly men" (Wis 1:16) who say, "Let us lie in wait for the righteous man, because he is inconvenient to us and opposes our actions" (Wis 2:12). And just as Jesus' direct challenge to the religious leaders leads to their plan to destroy Jesus, so, too, in the Wisdom of Solomon is the fate of the righteous man determined by his actions toward the ungodly:

> He reproaches us for sins against the law,
>   and accuses of sins against our training.
> He professes to have knowledge of God,
>   and calls himself a child of the Lord.
> He became a reproof of our thoughts . . .   (Wis 2:12–14).

And their reaction was to plan his death:

> Let us see if his words are true,
>   and let us test what will happen at the end of his life. . . .
> Let us condemn him to a shameful death . . .   (Wis 2:17, 20).

In this section of his gospel Mark has presented the story of the "beginning" of Jesus' ministry to Israel; his word has authority and the power to heal. Reactions to that ministry, however, are diverse: some, like Levi and the other disciples respond by a simple acceptance of Jesus' call to them and "follow him"; others seek out the good that Jesus can give to them but do not understand who he is and are "astonished" at the authority and power manifest in him; still others fully reject his call.

The *reader* of Mark's gospel, on the other hand, can not only know of these things but can interpret them in light of God's own testimony at Jesus' baptism. Jesus is the Righteous One, graced with the Spirit of God, Wisdom. His ministry is yet another instance of Wisdom's own ministry toward Israel. The reaction to Jesus' ministry was diverse, but so too were the reactions to Wisdom's own appeal. Some respond and "obtain friendship with God" (Wis 7:14; cf. 5:5; 7:16–18); others hear her call and do not respond (Prov 1:20–29); and yet others openly reject her, as did the ungodly men in the Wisdom of Solomon (Wis 5:6–7). Just as the rejection of the righteous man in the Wisdom of Solomon 2 is a rejection of God, leading to death (Wis 5:6–8) for the ungodly but vindication for the righteous man (Wis 5:1–5), so, too, the reader of Mark's gospel can anticipate, even as the Pharisees with the Herodians form a plan to destroy Jesus, the eventual vindication of Jesus. Even here, Jesus' resurrection is implied at the first intimation of his death.

The Description of the Righteous Man
(Wisdom of Solomon 1:16–2:1, 12–20)

1:16   The ungodly, however, in actions and speech invited death;
        ... because they are worthy of being in its company.

2:1   For they said to themselves, thinking incorrectly....

2:12   Let us lie in wait for the righteous man,
        because he is useless to us
           and opposes what we do
        and reproaches us for sins against the Law
        and charges us with sins against our training.

2:13   He proclaims to have knowledge of God
              and calls himself a child of the Lord.

2:14   He became for us the refutation of our ideas;
        even seeing him is oppressive to us,

2:15   because his life is unlike others'
           and his ways are completely different.

2:16   We are considered by him as something base,
        and he keeps away from our ways as from the unclean.

    He calls the final end of the righteous "blessed"
        and brags that his father is God.

2:17   Let us see whether his words are true,
        and let us test what happens at his departure;

2:18   for if the righteous one is a son of God,
           he will be protective of him
               and will rescue him from the hand of his
              opponents.

2:19   With wanton violence and torture let us afflict him,
        so that we may know his goodness
        and may test his forbearance.

2:20   To an ugly death let us condemn him,
        for, from what he says, he will be watched over.

2. The Second Interlude 3:7-19

Of Jesus, Disciples, and Mission

In just the brief narrative thus far Mark has already sketched the content of the "good news!": God brings to an end this old, historical order where men are under the curse of Adam's sin, subject to disease, and death, and sin, and the power of the demonic under Satan. In its place Jesus "comes" (note the references to that theme in 1:7, 9, 14 and especially: 1:38, 2:17) as the Son of God, graced by the Spirit and proclaiming that the kingdom of God is at hand, a new reality where his authority is absolute over those consequences of Adam's sin, and even over the requirements of the law through which Jews had sought to be "righteous." The people of Jesus' time, says Mark, stood at a juncture of history and allegiance. Their choice was simple, since the call was "to follow" Jesus into the kingdom. And so the plot is suggested and the characters are known. What the reader must yet discover is the eventual outcome of this dramatic confrontation between the old and the new, the demonic and Satan-controlled and the Son of God, the age of sin and disease and the kingdom of God. What the reader must also discover is what is required of anyone who would utter the cry of recognition, "You are the Holy One of God!" (1:24).

In 3:7-19 Mark reminds the reader of the key elements of the previous story, but especially the affirmation of Jesus as the "Son of God" (3:12) and the intimation of Jesus' death (3:19), while also indicating something of what discipleship requires.

These verses narrate two scenes; but that they were meant to be associated with each other is clear from the materials which precede it and which follow it: Mark 1:21-3:6 is bracketed by episodes located at "Capernaum," and Mark 3:20-6:13 opens and closes with episodes which describe Jesus' reception "at home" and speak of his mother and brothers and sisters. Hence Mark 3:7-19 separates two clearly identifiable textual units and functions as a major transitional unit. And like the previous paradigmatic transition in 1:16-20, it too will speak of discipleship.

The first part of this transition material is really a reprise of themes: Jesus is again "with his disciples" by "the sea." Not only they but "an enormous crowd . . . followed." Jesus' success has indeed drawn people "from all directions" (1:45), as Mark proudly relates in 3:7–8. The summary of his success (apart from 3:9) virtually mirrors the earlier summary in 1:32–34; indeed, the acclamation of Jesus as the "Son of God" by the unclean spirits (3:12) returns to their recognition of Jesus in 1:24 and reminds the reader once again of Mark's title (1:1) and of the testimony of the voice from heaven concerning Jesus (1:11).

As Mark continues his narrative, so great has been the response to Jesus that it seems only logical that Mark would show Jesus bringing others into the ministry to share his authority and to extend the proclamation of the kingdom to sinners. The core group of Peter and Andrew, James and John had already been enlarged by the addition of Levi, but there had been no effort to confer upon them a share in the responsibility for the spread of the kingdom. Until now that had been Jesus' role exclusively. But in the scene in 3:13–19 Jesus "called to himself those whom he wanted and they went to him" (vs. 13). Of this group he then chooses twelve to "be with him" (vs. 14), and he gives to them a share in his ministry, for they are to do what he has been doing: be sent out, preach, and cast out demons.

In 3:13–19, the list of the twelve is undoubtedly traditional material. Just as clearly, 3:13–14 are the transitional phrasing which Mark had to employ in order to move from the massive popular response of 3:7–12 into a setting where Jesus could choose a smaller group; that Jesus "went up into the hills" (vs. 13) does that. That the balance of vs. 13 is also a part of Mark's creation of a setting is likely because of its similarity with the theme of 1:16–20 and 3:13–14. Verse 14 is probably also part of the Markan framework because it describes the same role ascribed to Jesus in 1:39 and gives it now to the disciples, as does 6:7, 12–13. The effect of this framework material is to establish between the twelve and Jesus an intimacy of companionship and an identity of mission. Jesus and the twelve will now bring the proclamation of the kingdom of God to the people.

That intimacy of companionship and identity of mission again are reminiscent of the Wisdom tradition. The texts cited above in connection with Mark 1:16–20 are pertinent here as well.

What is most striking about this transitional piece, however, is the central position of the affirmation by the demons, "You are the Son of God!" (3:11). The reader knows, then, that it is Jesus, the Son of God, who

has "called to himself those whom he wanted"; and in the simple statement, "and they went to him," Mark sketches for the reader the fundamental element of discipleship: one must respond to the call to "be with"
Jesus, acknowledging him as the "Son of God."

That this material ends with the reference to "Judas Iscariot, who also
betrayed him" has three purposes. As the climactic element of this material, it anticipates that section of the gospel which narrates the betrayal of
Jesus, 14:10–15:39, and which begins with the words "Judas Iscariot, who
was one of the twelve, went to the chief priests in order to betray him." It
underscores, moreover, the tragedy of a disciple who would make the acknowledgement of Jesus as the "Son of God" and would then "also" turn
away from him. But the reference, secondly, serves to return the reader to
the ominous note with which Mark's preceding section had ended: the
plan of the Pharisees and the Herodians to destroy Jesus (3:6). And in
doing so, it suggests that discipleship and companionship with Jesus may
include the mission to preach and to expel demons (3:14), but it will surely
involve as well undergoing that same hostility and rejection which looms
ahead for Jesus.

C. Mark's Second Major Section 3:20–6:13

Of Response to Jesus, and Judgment

The clear intimations to the reader in 3:6 and 3:19 that not all acknowledged Jesus as the Spirit-graced Son of God nor "followed" him in response to his calling them prepare for the second major section of Mark's gospel in 3:20–6:13. Here Mark develops the theme of response to Jesus and of the consequences of that response, one's fate at the judgment. The responses are fundamentally two: conscious and explicit rejection of Jesus, on the one hand, and full and confident response to Jesus, on the other. These opposites are the extremes of "lack of faith" and of "faith," respectively, of "fear" or of *not* being afraid:

Rejection	*Acceptance*
associate Jesus with Beelzebul	associate Jesus with the Spirit
have a "lack of faith"	have "faith"
be "afraid"	*not* be "afraid"
not be given the secret of the kingdom of God	*be given* the secret of the kingdom of God
hear, but not understand	"hear" and "understand"

Yet they are the opposite ends of a *spectrum* of responses, as the parable of the sower and these various episodes will show; it is possible, for example, to be among Jesus' disciples but still be afraid and astonished, or to be like the woman with the flow of blood, full of faith but still afraid.

Nonetheless the two fundamental responses are clear, and in this respect, again, Mark is in harmony with the Jewish tradition's story about Wisdom. The Wisdom of God went about calling the simple and those without understanding to her; but not all responded, because some deliberately turned away. And so two groups emerged as a result of their response to Wisdom's call, the "foolish" or "unrighteous" (who rejected Wisdom's call) and the "wise" or "righteous" (who responded to her). And the ultimate fate of each group was determined by these fundamental responses to Wisdom, as the references indicate that we noted in the Introduction.

The book of the Wisdom of Solomon clearly draws the contrast between the two kinds of response in its portrayal of the "ungodly" (Wis 1:16–2:12; 2:17–24) and of the "righteous man" (Wis 2:12–16). But these follow an introductory passage in which a warning is given about the ultimate consequence of one's actions:

> For wisdom is a kindly spirit
>   and will not free a blasphemer from the guilt of his words;
> because God is witness of his inmost feelings,
>   and a true observer of his heart,
>   and a hearer of his tongue.
> Because the Spirit of the Lord has filled the world,
>   and that which holds all things together knows what is said;
> therefore no one who utters unrighteous things will escape notice,
>   and justice, when it punishes, will not pass him by.
> For inquiry will be made into the counsels of an ungodly man,
>   and a report of his words will come to the Lord,
>   to convict him of his lawless deeds . . .   (Wis 1:6–9).

And the fate of each basic response is also sketched:

> . . . he is found by those who do not put him to the test,
>   and manifests himself to those who do not distrust him.
> For perverse thoughts separate men from God,
>   and when his power is tested, it convicts the foolish   (Wis 1:2–3).

It is entirely appropriate, therefore, that the emphasis in the next episodes in Mark 3:20–6:13 is on the responses to Jesus and to the coming of the kingdom.

3:20–30   *Failing To Discern the Spirit in Jesus*

Mark in 3:20 suggests that, although Jesus has not sent the twelve away on their mission (they are present in 4:10 and 34, for example), the narrative will focus only on Jesus for a while: "he" went home, with no mention of disciples or the twelve. Mark sketches again the popular acclaim given to him by noting that "again a crowd gathered" (vs. 20). This provides a setting for Mark to introduce two misunderstandings of Jesus, who comes with the Spirit to proclaim in power and authority the new kingdom which God has called sinners to enter. "And learning about it, those who were close to him went out to restrain him" (vs. 21) because they think Jesus has gone a bit crazy. What the "it" might have been is a bit unclear; the context suggests only that Jesus' drawing the crowd led his friends to think his behavior to be bizarre and crazy. Perhaps a better clue is offered by the reaction in vs. 22; there the scribes accuse him of being possessed by Beelzebul because "he casts out demons." A glance at Matthew 12:22–23 and Luke 11:14–16 shows that those evangelists felt the need to report an exorcism of a demon, coincidentally in both cases, from a dumb man. And what follows in Mark 3:23–30 suggests also that some story of Jesus' casting out of demons must have been the "it" of Mark's reference in 3:21; perhaps the reference skips the paradigmatic episode in 3:13–19 and returns to the summary verses in 3:9–10, in which case the narrative line would continue smoothly.

In any event, Mark's focus is never in doubt: the charge is made that Jesus' activity is not of God but of "Beelzebul," that he extends the reign of Satan. The response in 3:23–26 shows how impossible that charge is: Jesus' activity destroys the power of Satan when he casts out demons; if he were part of the house of Beelzebul he would be attacking himself, as it were; Satan's kingdom would be divided, moving in two directions—demon-possession and demon-ousting—at the same time. And the conclusion is drawn in 3:27: since "no one can enter a strong man's house unless he first binds the strong man," Jesus has, in casting out demons, shown that the strong man/Satan has indeed been "bound" and the kingdom of God has come to "plunder his house" by freeing men from his power and from sin. The matter of understanding who Jesus is and what he represents is so critical that two more sayings are introduced to make the point that just about any "blasphemy" will be forgiven (vs. 28) except one, the denial of the Holy Spirit (vs. 29); since the scribes had refused to acknowledge Jesus' authority as the one who brings God's Spirit to men and identify that Spirit as its opposite (Satan), they were the blasphemers whose blasphemy is unforgivable, whose sin is eternal (vss. 29–30). Again we hear that either/or contrast so characteristic of the Jewish wisdom tradition; and in particular we hear again that ultimate rejection of a "blasphemer" of the Spirit from the Wisdom of Solomon 1:6.

3:31–35 Failing To Discern God's Will Before Natural Ties

The next episode Mark presents in 3:31–35 shows one other misunderstanding of Jesus. It is perfectly natural to expect that the bonds of family are strong and override the claims of others. When Jesus' mother and family arrive (vs. 31) they naturally expect an advantage of position and place nearer to Jesus because of the bonds of family. Jesus' response shows clearly that in the new kingdom of God, natural expectations are set aside; the bonds that matter are with God and the new relationship with Jesus is in terms of doing "the will of God." The kingdom of God is like a family, but the bonds of family relationship, of privilege and place, are accomplished through doing the will of God. Even Jesus' family have not understood this.

Mark has, therefore, in the scene which opens this section, picked up the theme of the rejection of Jesus implicit in the reference to Judas in 3:19: his friends "at home" think he is "beside himself" (vs. 21), the scribes think he is in league with the devil (vs. 22), and his family thinks that the old and natural bonds are still in place (vss. 31–32). Later the twelve will be presented by Mark as sensing something of the radically new which was "at hand," and their open response to Jesus' call had just been presented in 3:13–19. And thus the setting is complete for the parable of the sower and its interpretation and the parables of the kingdom which follow in 4:1–34.

4:1–5:43 A Section on Response to Jesus

Before examining the emphases of the material which begins at Mark 4:1, it would be helpful to notice three things:

(1) The material in 4:1–5:43 is organized as episodes which occur in the context of a boat journey. That journey is anticipated in 4:1–2 where the setting shows the crowd to be so large around Jesus that he gets into a boat and sits in it, teaching the crowd which stands on the shore; a similar picture is given in 5:21, the verse which introduces the final episode of the boat journey. The references in 4:35, 5:1–2, 5:18, and 5:21 detail the stages of the journey. The journey by boat serves to keep these materials together, to unify them.

(2) Throughout this unified collection of materials, Jesus is very much in focus and the disciples/twelve recede into the background. The disciples are not even mentioned in the setting provided for the parable discourse at 4:1 (and they haven't been mentioned since 3:19). They do reap-

pear in 4:10 and are referred to in 4:35. By implication, therefore, the disciples are the "they" in 4:35–5:36, but until the naming of Peter and James and John in 5:37 it is not at all emphasized that it is the disciples who have been accompanying Jesus. It is not until 6:1 that they reappear as a group.

(3) Finally, in this block of materials which begins with a parable about various degrees of a faith-response to Jesus (4:1–9, 13–20), there is a contrasting of faith/belief with fear/unbelief. If the disciples are those to whom it "has been given to know the secret of the kingdom of God," they are not yet entirely representative of the first kind of response, as 4:40 shows. The story of the woman with a flow of blood comes "fearful" (5:33) but also with "faith" (5:34), and the leader of the synagogue is urged "Do not be afraid; just have faith!" (5:36). Yet many take offense at Jesus (6:3), and he marvels at their "unbelief" (6:6). This is a section about *response* to who Jesus is, and the question is put as a challenge to the reader as well in 4:41, "Who then is this. . . ?"

4:1–20   The Parable of the Sower and Its Interpretation

The reader is accordingly not surprised to find Jesus teaching the crowds and the disciples about the meaning of the diverse reactions. The setting for this is given quickly in 4:1: "A very large crowd gathered about him so that he got into a boat and sat in it on the sea . . ." That setting is so quickly given that the reader moves immediately into the "teaching" (4:2) called the "parable of the sower" (4:3–8). In it, "seed" cast by the "sower" falls upon different kinds of ground; whether it grows depends upon how receptive that ground was, how ready it was to bring forth new growth/"grain." Some seed is "eaten"; other seed "withered away"; yet other seed is choked off; and, finally, some "fell onto good soil" and brought forth grain, in varying degrees of fruitfulness (4:8). The reader, of course, recognizes immediately the aptness of the parable because of the preceding context in Mark. Yet *in the narrative line,* the "crowd" of 4:1 would not necessarily have been aware of the events in 3:20–35 and might very easily have found this "teaching" obscure and difficult to understand. The appeal in 4:9, "He who has ears to hear, let him hear," suggests that two groups are emerging: those who can "hear" (in the sense of "under-stand") Jesus' teaching and those who can't.

Mark then presents a scene in 4:10–20 in which Jesus is alone with his disciples. Because to them "has been given the secret of the kingdom of God," Jesus will interpret the parable of the sower, leaving it clear which of the two groups they represent; the crowds, by default, are those who "hear and not understand" (4:12). And in his interpretation of the parable to his disciples, Jesus makes it clear that the parable was about the various responses to his own activity (in 3:20–35): he was the "sower" who, in his teaching/proclamation of the kingdom of God, "sows" the "word"; people respond to Jesus' bringing of this new reality God offers to men in different ways for different reasons, ranging from no response at all because of interference by Satan, to a short-lived allegiance because of the pressure of tribulation or persecution, to an allegiance which grows unproductive because of the distraction from cares of the world or because of the attractiveness of riches and material things, to, finally, an acceptance which is productive and bears fruit. The emphasis in 4:20 is scarcely different from 3:35: responding to Jesus' word and accepting it and bearing fruit are images of a complete personal commitment to the ethical activity enjoined upon those who will be in the "family" of God; they will do the "will of God." What that will of God is and what it requires, Mark has yet to describe to the reader. In 4:11 he calls it "the *secret* of the kingdom of God."

4:21–34   Other Parables of Response

There is no difference between the introductory phrasing in 4:13 before the interpretation of the parable of the sower and 4:21 and 4:24 which report two more sayings about two groups. On that slim evidence, the reader might assume that Jesus continues to address the disciples up to 4:25. Mark is not clear in telling the reader when he returns to a discourse to a crowd; that he does so is suggested by the fact that 4:26–29 and 4:30–32 are clearly parables ("the kingdom of God is like . . ."—4:26; "to what can we liken the kingdom of God?"—4:30) *without interpretations* and 4:33–34 suggests that Jesus is speaking again "to them," i.e. the crowds, "according to their ability to hear it." (If 4:26–29 and 4:30–32 were originally joined with the parable of the sower, there is a coherence of sorts: all are "seed" parables; it would have been Mark, then, who in 4:9–25, 33–34 introduced the theme of Jesus' privately explaining "everything" [4:34] to his disciples to whom "is given [to know] the secret of the kingdom of God" [4:11].)

It may very well be that Mark understood the sayings in 4:21–25 to have application to both the crowds and to the disciples. They are eschatological "warnings" and speak of the end-time when everything hidden and secret will be made manifest and open and when "the measure you give will be the measure you get." As warnings, their purpose is to exhort the "man who has ears to hear" (4:23) to respond generously: "For, he who has, it will be given to him; and he who has not, even what he has will be taken from him" (4:25).

The parables in 4:26–29 and 4:30–32 are "growth" parables in that they, in different ways, describe the growth of the kingdom of God. The first describes the kingdom of God as "seed" which grows *of itself* without the man who sows it knowing how. It is not, therefore, so much because of the man who sowed it that the kingdom grows, but because of the quality of the "soil" which "by itself bore fruit." But the growth has its term: "when the grain is ripe, he [the man] immediately sends out the sickle, because the harvest has come" (4:29). God, then, will at some point, when the kingdom has fully grown, bring the end-time, the "sickle" and the "harvest."

In the second parable (4:30–32), the "seed" image is specifically that of the smallest of seeds which will grow into the largest of all shrubs. Here the emphasis is on the enormous extent of the growth of the kingdom of God.

In the context of Mark's narrative line, therefore, the reader has seen that the challenge is clearly extended to the crowds. The "harvest"/"sickle"/end-time is ahead, and only those who have responded to Jesus' proclamation of the kingdom, accepted it and borne fruit will be finally included in it. Everyone is to "Understand what you hear!" (4:24) because it is not "given" to everyone to know the secret of the kingdom of God.

Mark closes off this first scene in the "boat journey" with his editorial comment on the material: "And with many such parables did he speak 'the word' to them, according to their ability to 'hear' it. Nor did he speak to them without using a parable, yet privately to his own disciples he explained everything" (4:33–34). Not only does this signal the end of Jesus' teaching the crowds "many things in parables" (4:2) but it turns the reader's attention back upon the disciples as a privileged group beside Jesus. It may very well have been the case that the core of these materials in 4:2–5:43 pre-existed Mark's writing of his gospel: it is striking that they focus upon the activities of Jesus and can be read as a coherent whole without the references to the "disciples" in 4:10–20, 33–34 and 5:31, 37, at least some of which are examples of Mark's redactional activity. In any event, the effect of 4:34 is to provide the antecedent needed for 4:35: it is the "disciples," you see, who will be the only witnesses to Jesus' "stilling of the storm" in 4:35–41.

4:35-41   The Question of Jesus' Identity

The reader of Mark's gospel is meant to understand that a close connection exists between Jesus' teaching in parables (4:2–34) and the stilling of the storm scene in 4:35–41. It happens on the same day, "toward evening" (4:35); it mentions the "crowd," on stage, as it were, since 4:1–2 and the "boat," last mentioned in 4:1; and when Jesus is awakened by his disciples in 4:38, he is addressed as "Teacher," a title appropriate after the references to Jesus' teaching in 4:1–2 and the paraphrase in 4:33. As we shall see, there exists another miracle story in Mark's gospel where Jesus is shown to have power over the natural element water, i.e. the "walking on the water" episode in 6:45–52; it, too, is closely associated with a preceding scene in which Jesus is "teaching" the crowds (6:34) and is intended to be understood in the light of that preceding episode (6:52). Mark here only suggests the connection between the stilling of the storm and the preceding scene in reporting Jesus' question in 4:40, "Why are you fearful? Do you not yet have faith?" Something, it seems, should have prepared "the disciples" to have understood that Jesus' "word" (4:33; cf. 4:14 and 2:2) was authoritative not only over disease and the demonic but also over the elements of the cosmos; the "faith" expected of the "disciples" to whom it had been "given" to know "the secret of the kingdom" (4:11) should have included an understanding, or "faith," concerning Jesus' own identity. You, dear reader, are privileged to have Mark's announcement in 1:1 and to have learned of the testimony of the voice from heaven in 1:11 and of the demons in 1:24. In the story Mark tells, however, the disciples have not had that advantage, and their reaction in 4:41—"Who then *is* this, that even the wind and sea obey him?"—is little different from the reactions of amazement and astonishment on the part of the crowds when the power of Jesus' word/teaching is displayed (that conjunction of teaching and authority/power in the word/teaching is announced by the Markan redaction in 1:27 where "they were all amazed"). That reaction of amazement and astonishment is here spoken of as being "afraid," an absence of the assurance of "faith" which would come from an understanding of who Jesus was. Mark tells his reader here that the disciples who walked with Jesus have not yet come to that point.

And yet Jesus' question in 4:40 suggests that there is something in the course of events which should have given to the disciples some indication of Jesus' identity, even though they do not share the knowledge the reader has. A Jewish audience, encountering this story of Jesus' curbing the wind and calming the sea, would have been reminded of the account of creation in Genesis 1 where God, with the power of his word, fashions an orderly cosmos out of the turbulent waters. The imperatives "Peace! Be still!" are also reminiscent of that absolute authority of God expressed in the imperatives "Let there be . . ." in the Genesis creation account. And, as we noted in the Introduction, Jewish wisdom literature could speak of God's creating the world through his Wisdom. What Mark suggests to his reader is that the disciples, in their seeing Jesus "teaching" (4:1–2, 33) about the "secret" of the kingdom of God (4:11) and in hearing him explaining "everything" (4:35) and in witnessing his authoritative word control even the elements of nature (4:35–41), should have made the identification: in Jesus, God's own Wisdom has come to Israel as its authoritative teacher, a theme which will be made even more explicit in Mark's next major section (6:30–8:21). In *this* section of his gospel, however, Mark's focus is not so much upon Jesus' identity as upon the *responses* made to Jesus.

5:1-20   Response to Jesus Outside Israel

As the boat journey continues, Jesus goes "into the region beyond the sea, into the territory of the Gerasenes" (5:1). It is probably not Mark's interest to provide his reader with an exact and detailed account of this "journey"; no time indications are given, and at last report it was "evening" (4:35), just before Jesus and those with him left by boat to go to the other side. And so we are left to imagine any chronological sequence we might choose, although the content of the story of the demoniac (he sees Jesus "from a distance"—5:6; people from the area are awake and able to react—5:14–15) suggests that it is the next day. The point Mark is interested in is missed, however, if we focus upon when this next scene happens. It is *where* it happens that is important, and Mark is quite clear about it: *Jesus has left Israel* and gone to the country of the Gerasenes (5:1), in the region of the Decapolis (5:20).

This scene in 5:1–20 is in many ways similar to another the reader has already witnessed in the gospel: Jesus' casting out of the unclean spirit in 1:23–28. There, when Jesus first opened his ministry to the Jews, the demonic world (note the *plural:* "What is there between us and you?"— 1:24) sensed the presence of one stronger than itself and cried out in recognition (1:24). Jesus silenced the demon and expelled him from the man. Everyone was "amazed" (1:27) and "at once his fame spread everywhere throughout all the surrounding region of Galilee" (1:28). Here in 5:1–20, Jesus is extending his authoritative presence beyond Israel; and even there, outside Israel, the demonic world (cf. 5:9: "My name is 'Legion,' because *we* are many") acknowledges the sovereignty of Jesus (cf. 5:19: "Lord") by worshiping him (5:6); after all, as the Wisdom of Solomon says, "the Spirit of the Lord has filled the world" (Wis 1:7). The question of the demon is also similar (compare 1:24 and 5:7) and in both cases is followed by a recognition of who Jesus is; here in 5:7, the demonic testimony is that Jesus is the "Son of the Most High God" (5:7). Then Jesus does not silence the demon but does give "them" permission to end their torment of the man they had possessed and the unclean spirits came out (5:13). In this story, the immediate reaction is *not* one of amazement but of *fear* (5:15); yet when the man who had been possessed "began to proclaim in the Decapolis how much Jesus had done for him . . . everyone wondered" (5:20), so that, in effect, Jesus' fame spread throughout this non-Jewish territory as it had earlier spread throughout all Galilee.

The story in 5:1–20 is delightful, filled with vivid detail (cf. 5:3–5, 11–13). That detail expresses the thoroughgoing power of the demonic in the non-Jewish world and provides the base-line for gauging Jesus' yet-far-greater power. It would be a mistake, however, to be distracted by that detail and to imagine it with the special effects of a Hollywood movie. Mark has told us clearly that in this part of his gospel he is sketching the various responses to Jesus' power and authority. Even in the non-Jewish world, the complete sovereignty of Jesus prompts acknowledgement by the demonic world and "fear" by the people who "came to see what it was that had happened" (5:14). This reaction by the people, coming as it does so soon after Jesus' question of those with him in the boat ("Why are you fearful? Do you not yet have faith?"—4:40), signals another interest of Mark in this section: the non-Jewish world is not given the opportunity at this time of having "faith." They can only be "afraid," which signals the absence of that understanding of and response to Jesus which is "faith"; indeed, when "the man who had been possessed with demons begged him that he might be with him" (5:18), Jesus "refused" him (5:19), and the non-Jewish world is left to marvel at the beneficence of "the Lord" (5:19).

5:21–43 *Response to Jesus Within Israel*

The final scene in this narrative of Jesus' boat journey is really two scenes, the raising to life of Jairus' daughter (5:22–24, 35–43) and the healing of a woman with a flow of blood (5:25–34). These two combine to illustrate the confidence in Jesus which "faith" is; as such this last scene of the boat journey contrasts with the preceding scene which illustrated the reaction of being "afraid" in the presence of Jesus, and these two scenes of chapter 5, therefore, together illustrate the meaning of Jesus' question to those with him in the boat in 4:40.

Again, the chronological relationship of this scene to the preceding is not important, but rather *where* it takes place: Jesus has "crossed again [in the boat] to the other side" (5:21); as is usual, a "huge crowd gathered" and Jesus is "beside the sea," a setting reminiscent of that which preceded the boat journey (cf. 4:1). Jesus is, presumably, *back in Jewish territory,* and the references to Jairus as a leader of the "synagogue" (5:22, 36) confirm this.

Jairus clearly exemplifies the quiet confidence of a man of faith: he falls at Jesus' feet, and asks Jesus to lay his hands on his dying daughter "so that she may be healed and live" (5:23). Even in the face of the impossible, he is urged by Jesus, "Do not be afraid; just have faith!" (5:36). For Jairus had been told that his daughter had in fact died—and told, indeed, by some who betray their own lack of understanding in calling Jesus "the Teacher," a title appropriate to this section but one with which those in the boat with Jesus had already betrayed their lack of full "faith" in and understanding of who Jesus is. This contrast of the believing, confident faith of Jairus and the uncomprehending response of others is continued when the people, "weeping and wailing loudly" (5:38) because the girl has died, *laugh* at Jesus (5:40). Jesus' response to "faith"/"belief" is to grant what is requested of him: he restores the girl to life and health, for she walks and is able to eat (5:41–43).

That the power of Jesus is accessible to those with faith is even more emphasized in the intervening story of the "woman who for twelve years had had a flow of blood, and who had suffered much under many doctors, and who had spent everything she had and who had in no way been helped, but rather had gotten worse" (5:25–26). (Whoever first described this fig-ure did so with a touch of humor and a sense that the more things change, the more they stay the same!) Her conviction is that a contact of any kind with Jesus' power will bring healing, and her simply touching his garments healed her (5:27, 29) because the "power had gone out" from Jesus (5:30). When called into the presence of Jesus (5:31), she came "fearful and trem-bling" (5:33). But Jesus tells her to "go in peace" because "your *faith* has saved you" (5:34). In her, therefore, as in the case of those in the boat with

Jesus during the storm, there is fear; but unlike that earlier portrayal, *her* fear is overcome by her "faith" in Jesus' power to make her well, and her "faith" does in fact make her well (5:29, 34).

The materials in 4:1–5:43, therefore, do narrow the variety of responses to Jesus shown in 3:13–35 down to principally two: that of "faith" and "belief" and those to whom it has been "given" to know the "secret of the kingdom of God," on the one hand, and that of "fear" (and "unbelief") and lack of comprehension by those "outside" (4:11) who do not "understand" (4:12), on the other hand. It is instructive to reread the interpretation of the parable of the sower (4:13–20) at this point: Jesus is the "sower" who in his presence and his proclamation/teaching of the kingdom of God "sows" the "word" or "seed." That seed *either* "immediately" does not sprout because Satan intervenes and "takes away 'the word' which has been sown in them" (4:15) *or* it sprouts and grows in various measures and outcomes (4:16–20). "Fear" and "amazement" are characteristic of the first kind of response; "fear" moving toward confident "faith" is characteristic of the second kind.

6:1–13   The Two Responses: Rejection and Discipleship

When Mark shows Jesus returning "to his home town" in 6:1, it provides an opportunity for him to emphasize the extent of "unbelief" (6:6) which had met Jesus. In his organization of the materials in 3:20–6:13, Mark here returns to the uncomprehending kind of responses he had earlier illustrated in 3:20–35. When Jesus teaches in the synagogue, the "many who were listening were astonished" (6:2); little has changed since Jesus opened his ministry in the synagogue in 1:21–22. When they question "How was wisdom given to this man?" (6:2), Mark's reader is reminded of his teaching in parables (4:1–34), and when they admire the "mighty works [which] happen at his hands," you think naturally of those remarkable episodes in chapter 5. And when they diminish his authority to the level of natural family ties, you remember the scene where he is "at home" (3:20) and his family came to him (3:31–35). "And they took offense at him" (6:3) *summarizes* simply the extensive failure to respond in "faith" to the "seed" which Jesus had sown in Israel. When Jesus says, "A prophet is not without honor, except in his home town, and among his own relatives, and in his own house" (6:4), the reader also remembers the similar references to "his home town" (6:1), his family (3:31) and his "house" (3:20). And Jesus can only marvel at their "lack of faith" (6:6a).

Mark had early-on prepared the reader for the outcome of Jesus' ministry with his report at the end of his first major section (1:21–3:6) that "the Pharisees went away, and immediately formed a plan with the Herodians against him in order that they might destroy him" (3:6). Now, at the end of this second major section of his gospel (3:20–6:13), Mark again intimates that the opposition to Jesus is intensifying; because of their "lack of faith," "he was unable to do any mighty work there" (6:5), except for healing a "few" sick people.

Mark closes out this second major section in 3:20–6:13 by a development of the scene in 3:13–19. There Jesus "established twelve [whom he also called apostles] that they might be with him and that he might send them to preach and to have authority to expel demons" (3:14–15). Here in 6:7–12 that mandate is pictured as actually being carried out in 6:7, 12–13: "And he called the twelve to himself and began to send them out, two by two, and he gave them power over the unclean spirits. . . . And they went out and preached that people should change their lives, and they cast out many demons and they anointed many sick persons with oil and healed them."

And thus this second section of Mark's gospel comes to a close. It had sketched two basic responses to Jesus, but it ended with the positive response of the disciples' own mission, both challenging directly the lack of faith which had met Jesus' ministry and at the same time challenging Mark's reader to decide whether Jesus is of Beelzebul (as the scribes had charged in 3:22) or of God. After all the section ends, as it had begun, with a direct confrontation of the demonic; in 3:20–30 Jesus had cast out demons, and in 6:7–13 Jesus gives that power to the twelve and "they cast out many demons." If Jesus had explained privately to his disciples (4:10–20) that the reason the "seed" which he had sown did not sprout was because "Satan" had "immediately" taken away the word which he had sown (4:15), Jesus, the authoritative one, now gives the twelve "authority over the unclean spirits" (6:7) and the cosmic struggle is thus enlarged as these twelve extend Jesus' ministry.

Conclusion

What 1:16–3:19 had portrayed as the "plot" and the "characters" in this cosmic drama is, therefore, developed in 3:20–6:13. In a unity of materials which has been accomplished through bracketing references to the casting out of demons, Mark again shows Jesus to be the one who brings the kingdom of God: in the wisdom of his teaching and in his authority over the demonic and disease, he is like a sower who broadly casts his seed. And again, there are fundamentally two responses: either to "follow" or not to "follow" him; in 3:20–6:13 the difference between the two responses, however, is described more fully in 4:1–5:43, which contrasts "faith" and "being afraid" or unbelief; and that series of episodes is bracketed by vignettes which contrast the response of "faith"/following with its opposite "unbelief"/being "afraid"/not following.

What has become more clear in this section is the extent to which entering the kingdom *depends upon "faith."* This new reality that God makes accessible to humankind is not without its challenge to us. Jesus had said in 1:15 in Mark's opening section, "Repent and believe in the good news!" He said that he came to "preach" (1:38) and to "call sinners" (2:17) in Mark's first major section. Now in this second major section he has described his work under the image of a sower sowing his seed, some of which will surely grow, without his knowing how (4:27), but with some growing more than others. What is important is this: "Do not be afraid; just have faith!" (5:36); your "faith" will make you well (5:34). So important is this faith response, this confident acknowledgement of Jesus' absolute authority, that not having faith closes men off from Jesus' "mighty works" (cf. 6:5).

The plundering of the strong man's (Satan's) house (3:27) has begun; it will continue in the work of the twelve who have been given a share in Jesus' authority (6:7–12). But the impression given by the earlier materials (1:16–20; 1:21–3:6; 3:7–19) that Jesus' ministry met with overwhelming popular success is here qualified: the popular reaction had been one of "astonishment," and "astonishment" is the lack of comprehension and understanding equivalent to "unbelief" (cf. 6:2, 3 and 6 where these ideas are brought together). And this section also suggests that it will not be soon that the kingdom will come in its fullness; the parables in 4:26–29 and 4:30–32 describe "growth," and growth takes time. There is also the active intervention of the "strong man," "Satan," who will not relinquish his control as easily as the demons and unclean spirits do: he "comes and takes away the word which is sown" (4:15). And so the dramatic confrontation of 1:16–3:12 between the old and the new, between the demonic and Satan-controlled and the Son of God/sower, between the age of sin and disease and the kingdom of God, continues in 3:20–6:13. What the reader has now learned in this latter material is how pivotal is the "faith" response. What the reader must yet learn is more precisely who Jesus is and, as we said before, what is required if that reader, is to utter the cry of recognition, "You are the Son of (the Most High) God" (3:12; 5:7). These topics will be the burden of the next two complexes of material in Mark.

3. The Third Interlude 6:14–29

The Baptist Who Gives His Life

The text of 6:14–29 presently stands as an apparently awkward intrusion into the narrative line of Mark's story about Jesus; continuity of the narrative would be better had, in fact, if one were to read 6:30ff immediately after 6:13. The awkwardness is evident both at the beginning and at the end. Mark 6:14 begins abruptly with the statement "King Herod heard about all this because his [Jesus'] name had become well known." What Herod had heard about is really unclear, since the preceding passage (6:6b–13) had focused upon the activity of the *twelve* and not upon Jesus. If the reference were to skip 6:6b–13 and go back to 6:1–6a where there are other reactions to Jesus, then the reactions in Mark 6:14–15 with their positive, though divided, appraisals of Jesus stand in tension with the negative appraisals in 6:2–3 which Jesus calls "lack of faith." The awkwardness at the end, in 6:29, occurs because the largest part of this material concerns the circumstances leading to the death of John the Baptist and the reaction of *his* disciples; and then in 6:29 it is the *Baptist's disciples* who take his body and lay it in a tomb. The narrative then abruptly resumes in 6:30, with no allusion to the story of the Baptist and his disciples, but with a description of the return of the "apostles" to Jesus.

Since these verses are part of the clear plan which shapes the whole gospel, however, it is necessary to think of Mark 6:14–29 as an integral part of Mark's composition. The association of the Baptist with Elijah was known to Matthew (cf. Mt 17:13), and in Mark the association is suggested in 9:13, "I tell you that Elijah has come, and they did to him whatever they pleased, *as it is written of him*," that is to say, as it is written here in Mark 6:14–29! The story of the death of the Baptist thus provides the literary antecedent to 9:13c.

Yet that anticipation of the allusion to Elijah in 9:13 would not seem to be enough of an explanation for the awkward positioning of the episode, nor would it be consistent with the other "interludes" we have examined thus far. Mark 1:16-20 suggests what discipleship entails: not just re-sponse to Jesus but a commitment to act consistently with it; Mark 3:7-19 shows, as we said before, that discipleship cannot be a passive thing, but must find its expression in being for others what Jesus himself was in his ministry. *This* interlude about the Baptist provides yet another illustra-tion of the implications of full discipleship.

When Herod hears about Jesus, he identifies him with the Baptist (6:16). The story, in narrating the circumstances which led to the death of John, emphasizes that "Herod was afraid of John, seeing him as a *righteous and holy man*" and that he "gladly listened to him" (6:20); the Baptist, moreover, was righteous and holy precisely because he announced what was "lawful" and consistent with God's will for men, even when it meant imprisonment (6:17-18) and eventually death (6:27) at the hands of a king who had the power to order it. That Herod should identify Jesus with the Baptist makes the Baptist and his fate a prefiguring of Jesus (as Mark 9:13 emphasizes), who came to Israel to teach how men should live (the thematic emphasis of Mark 6:30-8:21) and who would ultimately be put to death at the hands of yet another king (a part of the emphasis of 8:27-10:45).

If the interlude in 3:7-19 associated the disciples with the ministry of Jesus, this passage about the Baptist, in pre-figuring the death of Jesus, suggests that discipleship may very well include having to give up one's very life also. The Baptist, in not compromising what was "lawful" before God with what was desired by men, had to give his very life for that commitment. So, too, would Jesus. Can Jesus' disciples expect to give less than Jesus and the Baptist before him? Indeed, Jesus will tell his disciples in 8:35 that it is necessary to "lose" one's life in order to "save" it, and that in the context of Jesus' prediction of his own death in 8:31. In Mark 6:12-13 the disciples have begun to take up Jesus' own ministry: "they went out and preached that people should change their lives, and they cast out many demons, and they anointed many sick persons with oil and healed them." As the disciples take up Jesus' ministry, the reader should know that discipleship may also mean being called upon to confront the possibility, or even the reality, of death for the sake of the proclamation of the kingdom of God.

These verses in Mark 6:14-29, therefore, are yet another illustration of discipleship. The story of the Baptist's fate provides the extreme example of having to give one's life for one's commitment to the ministry of Jesus. And so this passage both refers back to the mission of the twelve in 6:12-

13 and extends the challenge of "response" to Jesus which was the theme of Mark 3:20–6:13: the Baptist's giving of his life for his commitment to the righteousness required by God is a lesson for the disciple of the full response to Jesus which the disciple must be willing to give. Moreover, by speaking of the Baptist as the teacher of how God wants men to live, this interlude anticipates 6:30–8:21, as we shall see. And by making John the one who prefigures Jesus, it anticipates both 8:27–10:45 and the passion narrative. Awkward these verses may seem, but they serve a function similar to the other "interludes" in this gospel: they say something about discipleship and they link major parts of the gospel narrative together.

D. Mark's Third Major Section 6:30–8:21

Jesus Comes to Israel as Its True Teacher

The story about the death of the Baptist (Mk 6:14–29), although it illustrated the full commitment expected of the disciples whom Jesus had empowered and sent out in 6:7–13, had left the questions of Mark 6:2 still to be answered: "From what source did these things come to this man? And how was wisdom given to this man...?" When Mark continues with his third major section of materials in 6:30–8:21, he indicates to his reader the *real* answer to that question: the Spirit which presenced itself in Jesus at the baptism (1:10) was the *Wisdom* of God, so that Jesus' ministry to Israel was that of Wisdom itself. As these episodes unfold, the clues Mark gives afford the *reader* the opportunity to make the association of Jesus with the Wisdom of God, even if Mark is careful to portray Jesus' disciples as not yet "understanding" this, since Jesus had not yet taught them the "secret" of the kingdom of heaven (he will do so in 8:27–10:45) nor been raised from the dead (9:9).

Mark 6:30–8:21 as a Literary Unit

But first let us look at an overview of the reasons for seeing 6:30–8:21 as a unified, literary composition. That unity seems to be clear because Jesus begins yet another "boat journey" in 6:32 and the theme of a journey by boat is abandoned in 8:21. That alone, however, is not enough to establish the unity of this material, since there are references to Jesus' geographical movement over land in 7:24 and 7:31. Rather, the overall unity seems most clearly established by the wording of 8:17–21 in which Jesus reminds the disciples of the feedings of the five thousand (8:19, referring to 6:35–44) and of the four thousand (8:20, referring to 8:1–10). It is further established by the concentration of the references to "bread" within 6:32–8:21; in fact, fifteen of the gospel's nineteen usages of that word occur here, and in several of those cases it is very clear that the usage is a metaphorical one, used to sustain a picture of Jesus as the Teacher par excellence whose abundant feeding of the multitudes and superiority over the elements of wind and sea should bring about "understanding." And a final, subsidiary argument may be made from the character of what follows in 8:22–10:52; if that material is redactionally organized by the bracketing function of the healing of a blind man stories (8:22–26; 10:46–52), then what precedes it must terminate at 8:21.

It should be noted that Mark's second "feeding story" (8:1–10) is virtually a duplicate of the first one in 6:35–44. It would appear that Mark has deliberately included the second "feeding story" in order to construct a concentric pattern:

A. 6:30–31 Jesus is alone with his disciples
 B. 6:32–34 First reference to the boat journey: many come to Jesus (33–34) and Jesus responds (34b–c)
  C. 6:35–44 Feeding of five thousand
   D. 6:45–52 Miracle on the sea, done privately for the disciples, with a closing reaction of astonishment
    E. 6:53–56 Widespread response to Jesus (54–56) after hearing of him (55); healing of many
     F. 7:1–23 In a controversy with Pharisees, over the eating of "bread," Jesus is shown to be the true Teacher of what God wills
    E' 7:24–30 Widespread response to Jesus (24) after hearing of him (25); exorcism of Greek woman's daughter
   D' 7:31–37 Miracle at the sea, done privately with a closing reaction of astonishment
  C' 8:1–10 Feeding of four thousand
 B' 8:11–13 Last reference to the boat (13) Pharisees come to Jesus and Jesus responds (8:12)
A' 8:14–21 Jesus is alone with his disciples

It is probably indicative of an earlier traditional pattern that the three initial episodes, i.e. the feeding of the five thousand, the walking on water, and the healings at Gennesaret (6:30–44; 6:45–52; 6:53–56), are paralleled in the same sequence in John's gospel (Jn 6:1–15; 6:16–21; 6:22–25). In central position, and therefore in a place of emphasis, Mark has placed an episode portraying Jesus as knowing what God had intended for the law, and so as the "true Teacher," in a dispute over the eating of "breads"; it is striking that John places at this point in the sequence his "bread of life" discourse in which Jesus is the "bread of life; he who comes to me shall not hunger, and he who believes in me shall never thirst" (Jn 6:35). It would appear that Mark has chosen to elaborate through the mechanic of a concentric structure what John had chosen to elaborate through an extended discourse of Jesus, the association of Jesus with the "bread of life," i.e. with the Wisdom which comes from God.

Jesus: Son of God and Wisdom of God

It is probably best to review, as background for this section of Mark's gospel, material from the Wisdom of Solomon before continuing. In that book from the wisdom tradition of Hellenistic Judaism one finds descriptions of the righteous man, who calls God his father and whom the ungodly call God's son, Solomon, and Wisdom herself.

If we were to begin with the first description given in the Wisdom of Solomon, that of the "righteous man," God's son, the following characteristics appear:

knowledge of God	Wis 2:13
knowledge of the law	Wis 2:12
warns men about sins	Wis 2:12, 16
offers blessings . . .	Wis 2:16
offers intimacy with God	Wis 2:16

But these are also the characteristics of Wisdom as she is described in this same book:

knowledge of God	Wis 8:4; 9:9–11, 17–18
knowledge of the law	Wis 6:17–18; 9:9
appeals to men to learn wisdom	Wis 6:13, 16
offers blessings/good things	Wis 7:11; 8:5; 9:18c
offers intimacy with self	Wis 6:12–13
and with God	Wis 7:14, 27–28

There is one difference between these two portrayals: the righteous man does not appeal to men to learn wisdom, and Wisdom does not warn men about sins (although this can be evidenced in Proverbs 1:23–31).

When Solomon is described, moreover, *all* of these characteristics are in evidence:

knowledge of God	Wis 7:15–22
knowledge of the law	Wis 6:17–20
appeals to men	Wis 6:1–11, 21–25
warns men about sins	Wis 6:4–8
offers blessings	Wis 6:10, 19–20
offers intimacy with self	Wis 7:13
and with God	Wis 7:14

What is at work in these portrayals is the principle expressed in Wisdom 7:27: "in every generation [Wisdom] passes into holy souls and makes them friends of God, and prophets." The reason that the portrayals of the righteous man and Solomon are so identical with that of Wisdom herself is because they are instances of those "holy souls" into whom the Wisdom of God has passed. Wisdom's presence in the righteous man/son of God and in Solomon caught them up into Wisdom's overarching appeal to Israel and to humankind generally to learn wisdom, i.e. what the will of God requires of humankind.

But this is what can be said also of Mark's portrait of Jesus; in place after place Jesus exhibits these same characteristics of the righteous son of God in whom Wisdom has presenced herself. If, then, the "Spirit" which was sent to Jesus by God at the baptism (it is God who sends Wisdom from on high [Wis 9:17] and who is the source of Wisdom [Wis 7:25–26]) was *Wisdom,* then Jesus also has been caught up in this same overarching appeal of Wisdom to Israel and to humankind. It is that association with the Wisdom of God which Mark now emphasizes in 6:30–8:21 and which is the special significance of Jesus' being God's beloved Son. Mark now gives an effective response to the questions of Mark 6:2, therefore: the fundamental source of Jesus' "wisdom" and "mighty works" is the presence of God's Wisdom in Jesus, the Son of God, who now comes to Israel as Israel's true Teacher of how men and women should live so as also to be righteous before God.

6:30–52

Mark provides an elaborate setting (6:30–34) for the story of Jesus' feeding a crowd of five thousand people. His narrative line, interrupted by 6:14–29, is resumed by the *return* of the apostles. In an effort to have some "rest," Jesus and the apostles then go away to "a deserted place" (6:31, 32) to be "alone" (6:32). But it was not to be: they were seen and recognized and "a huge crowd" (6:34) anticipated where they intended to go by boat (!) and ran "on foot" (!) to get there first (6:33). Even though Jesus can still call the place "deserted" (6:35) and speak of its remoteness (6:36), it is hardly now uncrowded.

Central to this setting is Mark's comment that Jesus' "heart went out to them, because they were like sheep without a shepherd; and he began to teach them many things" (6:34). If sheep need a shepherd for protection and guidance, Jesus' beginning to teach them suggests that the crowd is likened to sheep without a shepherd, not because it has wandered into a "deserted place," but because it does not have the teaching it needs for its protection and guidance. In other words, Mark presents Jesus as "the shepherd" who gives the guidance/teaching for which the people of Israel have a need so enormous as to occasion Jesus' compassion for them.

The disciples worry eventually that the crowd needs "something to eat" (6:36); when Jesus retorts that *they,* the disciples, should "feed them" (6:37), the disciples refocus that as "two hundred denarii worth of *bread*" (6:37). Although this exchange makes perfect sense, Mark, as we shall see, is working with the word "bread" as a metaphor for "teaching" about what God wants of men. And so this is the *first* instance of the disciples' *mis*understanding what was happening as Jesus taught the crowds: he was, in his teaching, feeding them with wisdom, the "bread of understanding," and truly giving them "something to eat"; the disciples, however, can only think of baked bread.

Jesus' response, then, was a challenge to the disciples who had just returned from "teaching" (cf. 6:30). When he tells them to give the crowd "something to eat" (6:37), he is telling them to teach, as he had been teaching. Missing the point, they think only of baked bread. And when Jesus asks them "How many loaves have you?" and they respond, "Five, and two fishes," Mark's Hellenistic Jewish Christian reader might well think of the five books of Moses which the Jews held sacred as their "law" and which could be summarized in the two commandments, "Love God" and "Love your neighbor." This is all the *disciples* had to give, but *Jesus* can take these and break them open, interpreting them according to the plan of God (cf. 7:8–13) and making them satisfy abundantly, so that what is available as "fragments" left over after all have eaten is even more than what had been there originally.

To read Mark's story as such an extended metaphor needs to be justified because the story does make "sense" on a literal level. Mark will not give away the second, "secret" level of interpretation or "understanding" even to his reader until 8:14–21 and the end of this section. But he does give a "clue" to what he is about in the next episode, which is intimately linked to the story of the feeding of the five thousand.

Mark shows that the story of Jesus' walking on the water (6:45–52) is to be linked closely with the story of Jesus' feeding the crowds abundantly in two ways: he has this episode follow "immediately" (6:45) afterward, and he introduces a narrative comment in 6:52 that relates the astonishment of the disciples to their failure to understand "the meaning of the loaves." Clearly Mark is speaking directly to his reader and noting that there was something about "the loaves" in 6:37–43 that the disciples *should* have understood, a second or "secret" level of insight and interpretation, which his reader ought also to have had.

Jesus' walking on the water is similar to the earlier stilling of the storm episode (4:35–41). There the connections with the creation account in Genesis 1 suggested that Jesus was being alluded to in ways that reflected Jewish speculation about the "Wisdom" of God. A Jewish-Christian audience would have been reminded of the connection between Wisdom's being the creator of the world (Prov 8:30; Wis 7:22) and the description of the world's having been fashioned from water and wind (Gen 1:2) and would have probably thought also of Proverbs 1:27–28, 33:

> When panic strikes you like a storm,
> and your calamity comes like a whirlwind,
> when distress and anguish come upon you,
> then they will call upon me,
> but I will not answer;
> they will seek me diligently
> but will not find me . . .
> but he who listens to me will dwell secure
> and will be at ease,
> without dread of evil.

Here in Mark 6:47–51, the scene seems even more to focus, indeed, upon that description of Proverbs and particularly upon the assurance of Proverbs 1:33, for when Jesus says, in the midst of adverse winds which have thrown the disciples into distress (4:48), that they should "Have courage!"

and not "be afraid" because *he* is there, he promises that sense of security and confidence in the presence of evil which Wisdom offers. Wisdom, moreover, also calls men to "come, eat of my bread" (Prov 9:5), and, in a different context, that is spoken of as the "bread of understanding" (Sir 15:3; cf. also Sir 6:19; 21:19–21). Mark, therefore, employs several elements in his narrative which, to a Jewish-Christian audience familiar with these images from Jewish wisdom literature, would have probably been recognized as allusions to the speculation which had developed around the figure of God's "Wisdom."

If Wisdom was thought to have been sent to Israel, to God's chosen people the Jews, in order to teach them what was pleasing to God (cf. Sir 24:8–12; Wis 9:10–11, 18), then these allusions set Jesus forth as Israel's "shepherd" (Mk 6:34) who has come to Israel as its true and authoritative teacher, to "feed" the people with a teaching that discloses "what is pleasing in thy [God's] sight, and what is right according to thy commandments" (Prov 9:9).

At this point the reader of the gospel can only suspect that this interpretation of Jesus in imagery drawn from the Wisdom speculation is what the disciples should have "understood" because of the abundant feeding of the crowd of five thousand as Jesus taught them what they needed. As the concentric structure develops and other materials sustain that imagery, the enormity of what Mark calls "the good news" can become more clearly understood: with Jesus' coming men have now the opportunity to learn the righteousness required by God and so to be saved (cf. Wis 9:10–18 again), to "dwell secure and . . . be at ease, without dread of evil" (Prov 1:33). It is no wonder, then, that Jesus reassures the disciples in 6:50: "Have courage! It is I. Don't be afraid!"

We should not leave the story of Jesus' walking on the water without noticing the way Mark describes the reaction of the disciples in 6:51–52: they were "extremely astonished" and without understanding, for "their comprehension was dulled." Although these are those whom Jesus had called and to whom the secret of the kingdom of God was being given, and those whom Jesus had empowered to extend his struggle against the demonic, they have in Mark's narrative line little understanding not only of what will be required of them ("discipleship" and its requirements are one focus of Mark's next and central section, 8:27–10:45) but also of who *Jesus* is. Mark has given his reader a marked advantage, and by the end of *this* section that reader will be yet more sure that Jesus is the one who is Israel's true Teacher of what God's commandment requires.

6:53–56

In the next episode Mark shows Jesus crossing by boat to a new location, Gennesaret, a bit south of Capernaum. Several familiar motifs from earlier materials in Mark's gospel are repeated: Jesus is immediately recognized and the sick are brought "on stretchers" (like the paralytic in 2:3–4) to wherever he was so that they might "simply touch the hem of his garment" (6:56, as the woman with the flow of blood had in 5:25–34, and as is mentioned also in 3:10). Those details were drawn from stories where Jesus responds to "faith" (2:5; 5:34), and Mark probably is suggesting that the attitude of "faith" is present here as well, although it is not explicitly mentioned. Instead the focus falls upon the climax in this transitional passage: "and as many as touched it were made well" (6:56).

There is in this scene no mention of the demonic, which needs to be cast out so that a person can be made well. Instead Jesus is "recognized" and sought out, and contact with Jesus makes the sick "well." If the larger context has thus far suggested that Mark is drawing upon the Jewish speculation about "Wisdom" in order to interpret who Jesus was for us, there is nothing in these verses to disturb that impression. After all, Wisdom "is found by those who seek her . . . he who rises early to seek her will have no difficulty" (Wis 6:12, 14) and "he who finds me finds life and obtains favor from the Lord" (Prov 8:35). The richness of blessings which Wisdom bestows upon those who seek and find her is usually expressed in terms of "wealth" or in terms of "wisdom" and "understanding." Still, in Sirach 2:16–18 there is also an image of *physical* well being:

> To fear the Lord is wisdom's full measure;
> she satisfies men with her fruits;
> she fills their whole house with desirable goods,
> and their storehouses with her produce.
> The fear of the Lord is the crown of wisdom,
> making peace and *perfect health* to flourish.

And in Wisdom 10:21, a verse that surely influenced Mark 7:37, the imagery says that

> wisdom opened the mouth of the dumb,
> and made the tongues of babes speak clearly.

Such was the inestimable value of Wisdom, therefore, that finding her brought a full range of blessings, even "perfect health." In his own way and in the context of a narrative of Jesus' ministry toward Israel, Mark has drawn a similar sketch of Jesus' inestimable power: "and as many as touched it were made well" (6:56).

If in his earlier sections Mark had presented Jesus as the Spirit-graced who enters into a cosmic struggle with the demonic in order to establish the kingdom of God, here in 6:30–8:21 Jesus possesses such a fullness of power that what was said of Wisdom may be said of him. If Wisdom can assert:

> Alone I have made the circuit of the vault of heaven
> and have walked in the depths of the abyss.
> In the waves of the sea, in the whole earth,
> and in every people and nation I have gotten a possession (Sir 24:5–6),

Jesus walks on the sea. If Wisdom says "Come, eat of my bread" (Prov 9:5) and promises that she "will feed him [the man who fears the Lord] with the bread of understanding, and give him the water of wisdom to drink" (Sir 15:3), Jesus feeds the crowd of five thousand. If Wisdom gives "life" and "perfect health," Jesus heals as many as reach out to touch him. The image of Jesus' coming to Israel as its authoritative teacher is sustained, therefore, from 6:30 to this point, preparing for a controversy with the Pharisees (7:1–23), which centers precisely on who it is who brings to the people an "understanding" of what the "commandment of God" requires.

7:1–23

When Mark brings his reader to this central passage in the section 6:30–8:21, he draws the sharpest possible contrast between Jesus' teaching which knows what the "commandment of God" (vs. 8) requires and the teaching of the Pharisees and scribes which is "invalidating the word of God" through their teaching (vs. 13). Although it is not always clear in the translations, Mark continues to employ his "bread" usages even here, for in the Markan framework the occasion which prompts the ensuing controversy is that the disciples are eating "breads" or "loaves" with unwashed hands. To a reader who has "understood" about "the loaves," this reference in 7:2 would, of course, signal the possibility of a "wisdom" orientation in what follows.

That Wisdom orientation is, indeed, emphasized both by the framework and by an expansion of traditional materials. In the framework material, besides the reference to "loaves" in 7:2, Mark has Jesus call the people to "understand" (vs. 14) and challenges the disciples for their lack of "understanding" (vs. 18). But the wisdom emphasis is clearest in 7:6–13 which has been inserted into an originally coherent controversy passage; the "Why do your disciples . . . eat bread with unclean hands?" question receives its response in 7:15 and its explanation in 7:18b–23, a tradition unified by the inclusion on "unclean" in 7:5 and 23. Since that question, however, involves a question of faithfulness to the Jewish rituals of purification, it also raises the matter of not living according to "the traditions of our forefathers" (7:5), which is the focus of 7:6–13. In that material, Jesus accuses "the Pharisees and the scribes" (7:5) of leaving the "commandment of God," of "invalidating the word of God," and this in the context of a basic commandment on honoring one's father and mother. The Isaian citation speaks of a "people" whose "heart is far from" God and who fail to know the righteousness that the commandments of God meant to establish among God's people, the Jews. The Pharisees and the scribes are indicted for failing to "understand" that it is what comes from the heart (7:20) that is crucial, because the heart is symbolically the source of one's commitment and action. Evil actions can defile a person (cf. 7:15, 20–21) and indicate that a person's "heart" is far from God. And the Pharisees and scribes, in insisting upon a slavish obedience to a traditional interpretation which is really contrary to the fourth commandment, completely miss the point that God's "word"/"commandment" sought to purify the heart, to make men and women righteous so that the honor and worship they would give to God would not be only "with their lips" and "in vain" hypocrisy, but would be true and effective.

The contrast is clear. The Pharisees and scribes know and observe only "the commandment of men" and make void the word of God. Jesus, on the other hand, knows the commandment of God and is able to discern what are mere "precepts of men." He is able to clarify what is fundamental, therefore. In his knowing what was the intention of the commandment of God, Jesus again shows himself to be like Wisdom, whose intimate association with the law of Moses is attested in Sirach 24, and

> who understands what is pleasing in thy [God's] sight and what is right according to thy commandments   (Wis 9:9)

(The context of Wisdom 9:13–17 is a similar contrast between the "counsel of God" or "what the Lord wills" and the worthless "reasoning of mortals.") In other words, Jesus is able to teach men "what pleases [God]" (Wis 9:18). And when in Mark 7:14 he called the people to him again and said to them, "Everyone listen to me and understand," he again utters Wisdom's call:

> To you, O men, I call ...
> Hear, for I will speak noble things ...   (Wis 8:4, 6).

Thus the central passage, 7:1–23, is so positioned and redacted by Mark as to highlight the association of Jesus with Wisdom which the earlier parts of this section have suggested: Jesus does what Wisdom does. The next passage sustains the theme even more sharply yet.

7:24–30

When Mark turns to the next episode he is careful to locate it outside the territory of Israel in "the region of Tyre"; that locale seemed appropriate for a story in which one of the characters is a non-Jew, a "Greek, a Syrophoenician by birth" (7:26). As is typical in Mark, Jesus "had entered a house and wanted no one to find out; but he could not escape notice" (7:24). With these brief comments Mark has set the stage for the healing story and its dialogue in which yet more clearly "bread" is a metaphor for that healing power which Jesus brings to Israel.

The situation in the main tradition involved a woman "whose daughter had an unclean spirit"; the woman now comes to Jesus and begs for an exorcism, and Jesus *refuses*. His reason for refusing is given in a metaphorical expression: "Let the *children* first be satisfied, for it is not right to take the bread of the children and throw it to the *dogs*" (7:27). The woman had not asked for "bread"; she had asked for an exercise of Jesus' authoritative power. Jesus is the one who refers to it as "bread." It is clear, then, that the dialogue intends to go beyond the literal story. The fundamental reason that the "bread"/exercise of authority and power cannot be granted the woman is that Jesus understands that the "children" must first be fed and she and even her "little daughter" are not "children" in the sense Jesus uses it. The response makes perfect sense, however, if "children" refers to the Jews, to Israel. The woman and her daughter are Greek, Syrophoenician "by birth" and outside the privileged group to whom the "bread" must first be fed; they belong to the other group, the "dogs" to whom it is "not right" to throw this "bread." When the woman responds in 7:28, calling Jesus her "Lord," she acknowledges that primacy of the Jews when she asks only for the "crumbs" which might fall "under the table." Because, then, the woman accedes to the divine plan that the "children"/ Jews must "first be satisfied," Jesus is able to respond to her request and to extend his authoritative power to her daughter, who is subsequently found to be free of the demon.

The story is of special interest because it sustains the use of "bread" as a metaphor for that which Jesus brings to Israel and because it continues, also, to draw upon imagery in the Jewish speculation about Wisdom. Like Wisdom, Jesus understands that his ministry is "first" to Israel:

> Then the creator of all things gave me a commandment,
>   and the one who created me assigned a place for my tent.
> And he said, "Make your dwelling in Jacob,
>   and in Israel receive your inheritance." . . .
> So I took root in an honored people,
>   in the portion of the Lord, who is their inheritance   (Sir 24:8, 12).

Like Wisdom, Jesus' role is to "satisfy" or "feed" the "children" with "bread." What is uncharacteristic of a Wisdom presentation, however, is that Jesus' feeding with "bread" is also a metaphor for his power which overcomes an "unclean spirit." Mark had, of course, right from the beginning combined the motifs of authoritative teaching and power over the demonic in the opening scene of the ministry, 1:21-28. Here in 7:25, 29-30 the demonic has receded to the background of this healing story: no demonic recognition occurs and Jesus has no need to silence the demon. As a consequence, the Wisdom allusions remain prominently in the foreground and serve to maintain the overall coherence of 6:30-8:21 in which Jesus, like Wisdom, comes to Israel as its *authoritative* Teacher.

7:31-37

There are several ways in which the next scene in 7:31-37 corresponds to its counterpart, 6:45-52, in the concentric pattern employed for 6:30-8:21; it again locates a miracle story at the sea, emphasizes that it is done privately, apart from the crowds, and closes with a reaction of astonishment. As part of the overall section it is not surprising to find that the healing of the deaf-mute would also suggest that Jesus is to be understood best in terms of the figure, Wisdom. The healing story in 7:32–35 is enclosed within framework materials which show Jesus returning to the Sea of Galilee, presumably in Israel, and after the healing enjoining a secrecy upon those who had seen it. That charge to silence is not obeyed, with the result that their astonishment at what Jesus does is put into words in 7:37.

This miracle is a double-healing because the man is both deaf and has difficulty with his speech; accordingly Jesus gives the man speech and hearing. In the reaction of astonishment this crowd of Jews says of Jesus: "He has done everything well; he even makes the deaf hear and the dumb speak." In this reaction one hears an echo of praises sung of Wisdom:

> Though she is but one, she can do all things,
>   and while remaining in herself, she *renews all things* (Wis 7:27).

> She reaches mightily from one end of the earth to the other, and *she orders all things well* (Wis 8:1).

> For she knows and understands *all things* (Wis 9:11a).

> because *wisdom opened the mouth of the dumb,*
>   and made the tongues of babes speak clearly (Wis 10:21).

And so Mark, with these various allusions to what had been said of Wisdom, draws out the significance of Jesus' teaching the crowd in 6:34. After the walking on the water in 6:45–52, the reader was challenged to "understand" something "about the loaves" and has now been given additional clues to the parallels between Jesus and Wisdom in succeeding passages. Now, when Mark turns to his next episode, the feeding of the four thousand, the scene is more than just a link in the concentric structure, looking back to 6:35–44: it is yet again a demonstration of Jesus' teaching/feeding Israel abundantly with the "bread of understanding."

8:1–10

The setting Mark provides in 8:1–2 for the feeding of the four thousand brings to mind immediately the scene narrated in 6:33–34. Indeed, the report of this miraculous feeding in 8:1–10 has many similarities with that earlier one in 6:33–44: Jesus has compassion upon the crowds; the disciples show their misunderstanding by raising the physical problem of feeding so many in the deserted place; Jesus asks "how many loaves do you have?"; he commands the crowd to sit down on the ground; Jesus takes the loaves; he blesses them; he breaks the loaves and "gave them to his disciples to serve" the people; fish are also distributed; "and they ate and were satisfied"; and they took up baskets of fragments; finally, the number of those present is mentioned. This second multiplication of "loaves" is so similar in so many ways to the first one that it would seem to be a retelling, or duplication, of it. Something like it would have been required by a concentric pattern, of course, and a concentric structuring of the materials might just explain why Mark includes another, almost identical, report of Jesus' multiplying the loaves to feed thousands of people, more than satisfying their hunger. (It is a curious thing that both Luke and John, who report the feeding of the five thousand, do not report the feeding of the four thousand. Luke, in fact, proceeds immediately from the feeding of the five thousand [Lk 9:10–17] to "Peter's confession" [Lk 9:18–22, par. Mk 8:27–30], thereby omitting *all* the material which suggests that "bread" is a metaphor for "teaching/authority/power" and that Jesus could be interpreted as the "Wisdom" of God.) Whatever assessment one makes of Mark 8:1–10, it certainly stands as part of a whole in Mark's mind, as 8:19–20 indicate. And to the reader who has noted the ways in which Jesus parallels the portrayal of the Wisdom of God, the second feeding story simply confirms that impression, particularly after the metaphorical use of bread in 7:27–28 and the clues offered to Jesus' identity in 7:27a and 7:37.

8:11–13

When Mark's reader comes to the short scene in 8:11–13, therefore, the refusal of Jesus (8:12) to grant a "sign from heaven" as the Pharisees had requested (8:11) is completely understandable. This series of episodes which began at 6:35 is one long "sign," and the Pharisees' inability to recognize the sign, indeed, their desire to "test" him (8:11), puts them assuredly among the unbelievers. It was the Pharisees, you will remember, who did not know the "commandment of God" but only the "tradition of men" (7:8). What the Pharisees request is a "proof" on which to base their faith, a "sign" from above and separate from Jesus. The request is a self-indictment of the Pharisees, for in Mark's presentation *Jesus himself* is the "sign from heaven," *God's Wisdom come to Israel* to show compassion upon a people without a shepherd by feeding them abundantly with the bread of understanding.

8:14–21

And so, Mark's reader has come in 8:14–21 to the end of this concentric structure where are given the most obvious indications both of the unity of 6:30–8:21 but also of there being a level of interpretation which is both beyond the literal and intended by Mark. The reference in 8:19–20 looks back not only to the last feeding story but also to the first. And the questioning of the disciples in 8:17 ("Do you not yet perceive or understand. . . ?") and 8:18 ("Having eyes do you not see. . . ?") culminates in 8:21, "Do you not *yet* understand?" The vehement questioning about the *disciples'* understanding was occasioned again by a usage of "bread" as a metaphor. In 8:14 the disciples "had forgotten to take bread along and, except for one loaf, they did not have any with them in the boat"; the apparently contradictory saying makes sense if the "loaf" is *not* baked bread, but Jesus whose teaching has been referred to earlier as "bread." When Jesus cautions the disciples in 8:15 to "beware of the leaven of Herod," the disciples understand it to refer to baked bread (8:16, "we have no *bread*"); but Jesus explicitly *rejects* that linkage in 8:17. "Leaven" is *not* "bread," therefore, but stands for something else, as did the "loaves" in the two feeding stories (thus 8:17–21).

Mark had challenged his reader in a narrative comment to "understand" what the disciples did not after Jesus walked on the water (6:52); his reader is now again challenged, and this time by Jesus himself to "understand" something about the loaves that will indicate who Jesus is (8:17, 21). Mark's narrative has now returned to the setting with which it began: the disciples, alone, with Jesus, in a boat (cf. 8:13; 6:31–32). During this "second" journey by boat, Mark has concentrated upon materials that "see" (8:18) Jesus through the filter of Jewish speculation about Wisdom. If you have "understood" that second level of interpretation and have learned one answer to the question of "who Jesus is," what remains is for Mark to deepen that understanding and to plainly relate what is required of those who would follow Jesus as his disciples. That is the focus of Mark's next and central section, 8:27–10:45, to which we will soon turn. But first, Jesus who opened the mouth of the dumb will also give sight to a blind man (8:22–26), enabling him to "see" clearly.

4. The Fourth Interlude 8:22–26

The Healing of a Blind Man

Once again the narrative progress of the gospel is interrupted for an episode that offers a lesson in discipleship. When the preceding section (6:30–8:21) came to its climax, Mark's reader had seen Jesus giving expression to his exasperation at the failure of the disciples to "understand" the significance of the feeding of the crowds of thousands with a few loaves of "bread." It was as though they were blind men; Jesus says of them, "Having eyes, do you not see?" (8:18). Mark's reader knows that the disciples are, in fact, *doubly* blind, for they have "not yet" perceived that Jesus is the Son of God graced with the Wisdom of God, nor have they yet learned what the "secret of the kingdom" is. The remarkable account of the healing of a blind man not coincidentally restores sight in two stages, just as blindness to the real identity of Jesus must be overcome before a natural human blindness and resistance to Jesus' teaching about the kingdom can be.

In this episode, the disciples continue to accompany Jesus as they had in the preceding verses, but they quickly disappear from the scene as the story of the blind man begins. Some "people" bring a blind man to Jesus, and then the episode continues with only Jesus and the blind man in view (8:23–26). The "blind man" in effect replaces the disciples who "having eyes do . . . not see" in the narrative line (the "disciples" will reappear in 8:27). In this episode Mark's reader will learn what it will require to overcome their blindness.

Mark's report of Jesus' healing a blind man at Bethsaida (8:22–26) occurs nowhere else in the gospel tradition. It is a remarkable account because the miracle happens in stages, as it were, reluctantly. The other motifs are often enough found: people brought the man to Jesus; they begged him to touch him. If Jesus' leading the man out of the village and his later instruction "Do not even go into the village" (8:26) are seen as efforts at secrecy, these also have their counterparts in Mark's gospel. But the use of spittle on the eyes *is* unusual, and the necessity for Jesus to then lay his hands upon the man's eyes in order for his sight to be restored completely is *certainly* unusual. This is the same Jesus whose power is such that the mere touch of his garment heals, a detail from the story of the woman with a flow of blood (5:25–34) which Mark emphasizes elsewhere (3:10; 6:56), and this is the same Jesus who can silence demons and wind and sea by speaking a word. That here he cannot seem to heal this blind man immediately is unusual enough to draw our attention.

Elsewhere Mark had suggested that Jesus' healing power was effective in proportion to the faith of those who petition him. In that same story of the woman with the flow of blood, for example, Jesus explains to her, "Daughter, your faith has saved you!" (5:34). Then again, when Jesus is rejected, Mark tells us that Jesus "was unable to do any mighty work there . . . and he marveled at their lack of faith" (6:5–6). That understanding of the importance of the individual's faith for Jesus' healing power to be effective probably explains the unusual miracle account here in 8:22–26. Jesus has led the blind man away from those who had brought him forward; the faith of the crowd cannot substitute for the man's own response to Jesus. That the miracle didn't happen completely and immediately suggests that the man's faith in Jesus was less than perfect. There is a measure of physical healing because now the man can see other men, yet he sees them as "walking trees" (8:24). To the man of faith, others without faith are "dead" and "without life"; to this man once blind, having his sight restored to see men as but "walking trees" indicates a beginning faith. The emphasis in the story falls upon the consequence of Jesus' laying his hands upon him a second time: "the man opened his eyes and was well again and he looked at everything clearly" (8:25), just as the person of faith "sees" and "understands."

Coming as it does just after Jesus' reproach to the disciples in 8:18—"Having eyes, do you not see. . . ?"—this miracle story is a parable of the disciple who moves from an incipient belief to full belief. The parable of the sower had sketched various kinds of response to Jesus; the disciples themselves are examples of followers of Jesus with a faith that must develop, for they, too, can be "astonished" and "afraid," indicators of a lack of full faith. The man whose daughter has died is also an example: "I believe; help my unbelief!" (9:24). Faith, then, is a spectrum, moving from an incipient faith (not much different from "unbelief" and shown as such by reactions of fear) to complete faith (in which one looks at "everything clearly" [8:25]).

This story is very appropriately placed, therefore. It comes *after* 6:30–8:21 where the disciples are challenged to "understand" something about the *significance* of the events related there. Failure to perceive that in Jesus God's Wisdom has come to Israel is a "blindness" which sees things at one (human) level and not at their level of significance in God's plan; the blind man received his physical sight, but still saw things unclearly: "I see (men) like walking trees"; but then he subsequently "looked at everything clearly." Thus the progression of a disciple from blindness to partial faith to the assurance of complete faith is illustrated here (as it had been earlier in the parable of the sower), a progression indicated also by the challenge to the disciples in the preceding section, 6:30–8:21.

The story is also appropriately placed *before* 8:27–10:45, 46–52 because in that material the "secret" of the kingdom of God will be shown to be a *reversal* of all human expectations. What will be disclosed there is a way of living which must appear to men unnatural and impossible, but which to the disciple who sees "everything clearly" is the will of God for men. That "secret" involves the acceptance of the necessity of denying oneself, of putting oneself at the service of others, of opening oneself up to even the least of those who live in community with us. These words challenge us today at least as much as they would have challenged Mark's first audience.

That man once blind, therefore, is also a figure of Mark's reader in every age, and of all men and women who approach toward the wisdom of God: understanding of God's plan for men, clear sight of "everything," is possible only *through* Christ and only after the blindness which accepts only the natural and the human has been stripped away. And how is such blindness finally to be overcome?

The episode in 8:22–26 shows that it is by Jesus' action that blindness is finally overcome, but it is not independent of one's own initiative either. If in 6:5–6 Jesus "could do no mighty work there . . . because of their unbelief," so too here Jesus encounters difficulty. The "faith" of the "people" who brought the blind man to Jesus occasions Jesus' effort to heal him, but it is not immediately successful. Without his own full faith response, the blind man can only perceive things in a clouded, hazy way: "I see men; I see them like walking trees" (8:24). It is not until the blind man "opened his eyes" that he "was well again and looked at everything clearly" (8:25). Because the blind man responded to Jesus' initiative with his own effort to see things clearly, Jesus' outreach toward him ("then again he laid his hands upon the man's eyes," vs. 25) becomes effective in overcoming his blindness.

The episode in 8:22–26 has also served to reassure the reader of Mark's gospel: the disciples' blindness *will* be removed, and by Jesus' action at some time in the future. What Jesus' disciples (in every century!) need is for Jesus to *continue* his efforts with them; then they too will eventually "see clearly." In Mark 8:27–10:45 more of that "blindness" and failure to understand is set aside, at least for the reader, as Jesus begins to teach the disciples about what is "of God."

In 8:26 there is a curious ending to the episode: "he sent him away to his home, saying, 'Do not even go into the village.' " The man who was blind but who now sees clearly cannot become part of the group which follows Jesus in the gospel of Mark, for those disciples don't yet see and won't until after their experience of Jesus as risen. This episode pre-figures that outcome of faith on the part of the disciples, but it is not how they are responding to Jesus presently, and the man who now sees "everything" clearly cannot be part of them.

This "interlude," therefore, like the others looks backward (to the situation of the disciples' blindness in 8:18) and forward (to Jesus' continued teaching of the disciples in 8:27–10:45 and to the disciples' eventual faith after the resurrection). It also concerns discipleship in that it shows that Jesus' outreach is most effective only when those addressed by Jesus themselves make an effort to respond: one cannot "see" "everything clearly" until one has "opened his eyes."

E. Mark's Central Section 8:27–10:45

The "Secret" Wisdom and True Response to God: Giving All, to All, Gains All

In Mark 8:27–10:45, the central section of Mark's concentric plan for his gospel, the thematic emphases of the gospel all come to expression. The question of Jesus' identity is clarified, and the voice from heaven attests to Jesus' being God's "beloved Son" and the one whose authoritative teaching alone we should listen to (9:7). The "secret of the kingdom of God" (4:11) is disclosed: Jesus and those who follow him "must" (8:31) give of themselves in the service of others (10:43–45), for this is what is "of God" (8:33). And the "good news" is that this obedience to the wisdom and will of God leads to resurrection for Jesus (8:31; 9:31; 10:34) and "eternal life" (10:17, 30) for those who follow him.

One element of the blindness of the disciples had been their failure to perceive the real identity of Jesus. After Jesus stilled the storm they asked, "Who then *is* this. . . ?" (4:41). They contribute no answer to the questions of the townspeople in 6:2, "From what source did these things come to this man? And how was wisdom given to this man, and how do such mighty works happen at his hands?" Their behavior throughout 6:30–8:21 shows their failure to "understand" who Jesus is and what that implies; Mark tells his reader in 6:52 that "they had not understood the meaning of the loaves," and the closing scene ends with Jesus' impatient "Don't you *yet* understand?" (8:21). When the narrative line continues in 8:27 (after the interlude in 8:22–26), the question of Jesus' identity is sharply put by Jesus himself. It is clear that he expects a *different* response from his disciples (8:29) than from people generally (8:27). Mark's reader can only be skeptical, after all the evidence of the disciples' failure to "understand"

and particularly after 8:21, that Peter's quick response (8:29) is any more on target than the responses offered in 8:28. Jesus' rejection of it in 8:30 and his rejection in 8:33 of Peter's understanding of it confirm the fact that the blindness of the disciples to Jesus' real identity continues. It will take a revelation from heaven in 9:7 to identify Jesus as God's "beloved Son" for them. And yet, as we shall see, their continued misunderstanding of what Jesus teaches in 8:31 and 8:34–35 is apparent as the gospel continues and suggests that even God's own testimony did not entirely remove their blindness. Truly they are like the blind man in 8:22–26 whose sight could not be restored immediately.

It is at this point that Mark discloses to the disciples and to his reader what is the "secret" of the kingdom of God: it is God's will for men and women that they should be at the service of one another. This was the "wisdom" the people of Israel had sought and which Jesus, graced by the Wisdom of God, had come to Israel to teach. Such was Jesus' own understanding of what was required of him, as it is expressed both in the first prediction of the passion (8:31) and in the climactic saying of this section: "The Son of Man did not come to be served but to serve" (10:45). It was even *required* (8:31) that the Son of Man must "give his life" (10:45). This teaching of Jesus is a clear reversal of human expectations (10:31; 10:43–44) and the disciples recognize it as such (10:26). But Jesus' teaching is clear: "whoever wants to save his life will lose it; and whoever loses his life because of me and because of the good news *will save* it" (8:35). In Mark 8:31 (and again at 9:31 and 10:33–34), the prediction Jesus makes of his own suffering leads inevitably to his confident affirmation of the immortality every righteous man hopes for, a continuance beyond death, a resurrection: "and after three days [he will] rise again!" *This* is the true climax: the assurance that one's giving of oneself in service to others—the "secret wisdom" of God which Jesus taught—gives resurrection and eternal life.

Mark here gives his reader a narrative section which so emphasizes the uniqueness of the follower of Jesus in terms of a letting go of the desire to control one's own rise to prominence and prestige (10:35–45), in terms of service of others, in terms of "denying" himself (8:34), that it expresses the essence of the "love" ethic of Matthew's gospel and of the "community" ethic of the letters of Paul. Mark accomplishes this in a series of scenes in which the *meaning* of Jesus' own ministry, ending as it will in his death, is said "openly" (8:32) to the disciples. Their failure to understand provides the opportunity for Jesus to explain that fundamental meaning under various images, as we shall see. But the three predictions of the passion, death, and resurrection of Jesus (8:31; 9:31; 10:33) are the principal means of illustrating God's will for man: if even the Son of Man, God's judge, first in honor and full of power over all creation, God's own beloved Son, "*must*" (8:31) suffer and die, Jesus himself becomes the parable expressing what God wants of humankind. It is often said that Mark's gospel is a "passion narrative" with a long introduction. It would be more precise to say that Mark explains the passion narrative's meaning, for those who have eyes to see it, as calling Jesus' disciples to a taking up of the cross, a denial of self. This is what is "of God," and it is clearly not what is "of men."

Mark 8:27–10:47 in an Overview

a. 8:27–30 What the disciples say about Jesus (Son of Man)
  b. 8:31–33 **Resurrection prediction and incomprehension**
    c. 8:34–9:1 Death to self, **for Jesus and gospel,** necessary to **enter kingdom of God**
      d. 9:2–8 On listening to Jesus
        e. 9:9–13 Jesus alone with disciples, answers question
          f. 9:14–15 Crowds run to Jesus; scribes argue
            g. 9:16–27 Of demons and faith
              h. 9:28–29 Jesus alone with disciples
                i. 9:30–32 **Resurrection prediction and incomprehension**
              h′ 9:33–37 Jesus alone with disciples
            g′ 9:38–50 Of demons and faith
          f′ 10:1–9 Crowds gather to Jesus; Pharisees test
        e′ 10:10–12 Jesus alone with disciples, answers question
      d′ 10:13–16 On coming to Jesus
    c′ 10:17–31 Giving up one's goods, **for Jesus and gospel,** necessary to **enter kingdom of God**
  b′ 10:32–40 **Resurrection prediction and incomprehension**
a′ 10:41–45 What the disciples must do to imitate Son of Man

The narrative section in which Mark thus interprets the meaning of Jesus' death, and explains what true discipleship entails, is a carefully composed, concentrically organized piece. There are careful indications of changes of scene, of correspondences between parts, and—especially—of repeated predictions of Jesus' passion which are misunderstood by the disciples and then explained. Before and after all these materials on true discipleship are two healings of blind men (8:22–26; 10:46–52), each of which represents both the blindness which must be overcome if one is to become the follower of Jesus and the clear vision which should characterize that disciple. What Jesus teaches—in word and in his own death—as necessary if one is to enter into the kingdom of God is by every human estimation foolishness and impossible; to react in this way and to fail to see it as God's will is a "blindness" which only an appeal to Jesus himself can overcome; it is he who gives "eyes to see" to the disciple.

Mark 8:27–10:45 stands in central position in the overall plan of the gospel, therefore. As the central section of the concentric structure given to the parts of the gospel, it explains what to Mark's reader had remained unclear in the first half (i.e. what was the "secret" requirement for entering the kingdom of God) and it anticipates the second half (because Jesus' *cross* becomes a paradigm for true discipleship). Here is where the reader will find Mark's "theology of the cross" focused and explained; the Christian does not suffer physical distress for the sake of suffering but rather accepts it because physical suffering is but one variant of that denial of oneself required if one is to love another human being and be a "slave" (10:44), at the service of another.

Before examining the way in which Mark presents these themes through the individual passages of 8:27–10:45, it is perhaps useful to note briefly the general indications which support the idea that this section is a deliberately composed, concentric structure. There is, of course, the general focus on discipleship in 8:27–10:45, which emphasis comes at least partly from the fact that about one-third of the usages of "disciple" occur here (thirteen out of forty-five occasions). Moreover, Mark 10:46–52 has the character of a "call of a disciple" story and would, with 8:22–26, create an effective bracketing for material on discipleship. But it is the careful indications of changes of scene and development in the narrative which show best how Mark composed this section: 8:22, 27, 34; 9:2, 9, 14, 15, 28, 30, 31, 33; 10:1, 10, 13, 17, 32, 46. When the paralleling first and third predictions of Jesus' passion, death, and confirming resurrection are inserted, the *second* prediction falls at the mid-point of these materials and the following concentric structure can be seen, as the next page illustrates. This concentric structure is reinforced by formal correspondences between the parts of the structure and by correspondences of content.

[8:22–26 A blind man receives his sight]

  a. 8:27–30 The contrast between what people say about Jesus and what the disci-
          ples say

    b. 8:31–32a, A *resurrection prediction,* an uncomprehending reaction by the dis-
       32b–33 ciples, corrected by Jesus

      c. 8:34–9:1 The necessity of death to self ("cross"), *for Jesus and the gospel,* in
              order to *enter the kingdom of God*

        d. 9:2–8 The blessedness of Jesus the Son

          e. 9:9–13 Jesus interprets the scriptures, against the scribes, for the disci-
              ples, privately

           f. 9:14–15 The crowds acclaim Jesus, but the scribes are hostile

            g. 9:16–27 Jesus *casts out* an unclean spirit in response to *faith,* in a faith-
               less age

             h. 9:28–29 Jesus, alone with the disciples, in a house, deals with their
                 failure (to cast out spirits)

              i. 9:30–32 A *resurrection prediction,* and the disciples' misunderstand-
                ing reaction

             h′ 9:33–37 Jesus, alone with the disciples, in a house, deals with their
                failure (to understand the need to give up personal ambition,
                self-assertion)

            g′ 9:38–50 Jesus permits others to *cast out* demons; speaks of *faith* and of
              scandalizing that faith

           f′ 10:1–9 The crowds acclaim Jesus, but the Pharisees test Jesus

          e′ 10:10–12 Jesus interprets the scriptures, against the Pharisees, for the
             disciples, privately

        d′ 10:13–16 The blessedness of all who become like children

      c′ 10:17–31 The necessity of giving up what one owns, *for Jesus and the gospel,*
           in order to *enter the kingdom of God*

    b′ 10:32–34, A *resurrection prediction,* an uncomprehending reaction by disci-
       35–40 ples, corrected by Jesus

a′ 10:41–45 The contrast between what people do and what the disciples must do

[10:46–52 A blind man receives his sight]

*8:27–30   What People Say About Jesus
and What the Disciples Say*

    After the healing of the blind man, Mark moves into the central section
of his gospel, 8:27–10:45, by again challenging both the disciples and his
reader. In 8:27 Mark shows a change of scene to indicate the new material
and he then introduces Jesus' question: "Who do people say that I am?"
(8:27). The disciples give various responses: John the Baptist; Elijah; one

of the prophets. And then the challenge is put: "But *you*, who do *you* say that I am?" (8:29), to which Peter replies, "You are the Christ!"

Many authors are so impressed by this confession of Peter that they see this as a turning point in the gospel. They interpret Jesus' instruction in 8:30 to be "to tell no one about him" part of the effort Jesus supposedly makes to keep his identity secret, and they see 8:31 and Jesus' "beginning to teach" his disciples as a reward of sorts for Peter's correctly identifying who Jesus is. Such an interpretation makes too much of Peter's response in 8:29, as the episodes in 8:32–33 and 9:5–8 will show clearly. Peter's faith has *not* advanced to the point where it is "of God" (8:33), even if he has happened upon a title for Jesus which Jesus will subsequently affirm when it is conjoined with and modified by "Son of God" (14:62; cf. 1:1). In any event, this is an episode which concerns the identity of Jesus and the disciples' faith response to Jesus.

8:31–33 *A Resurrection Prediction, a Misunderstanding, and a Correction*

In 8:31 the reader encounters the first so-called "passion prediction" in which Jesus actually looks with confidence beyond his passion and death to the confirming climax of his resurrection. Given the intimation in 3:6, the reader is not surprised to find Jesus himself anticipating his death. But there is *plenty* to be surprised at. For one thing, Jesus begins to use the title "Son of Man" for himself in this very context of his death. The Son of Man was traditionally thought of as God's judge, sent from on high at the end of time to punish the evil and gather the righteous elect into God's kingdom. To speak of him as *suffering* and being *killed* was a startling reversal of that traditional conception. Moreover, Jesus' words speak of that suffering and dying of the Son of Man as a *necessity;* he *must* do so, i.e. because it is *God's* plan for Jesus/beloved Son/Son of Man. Finally, Mark's reader would have been struck by the climax of the prediction, "after three days *rise again.*" This expresses the conviction of Jesus' own individual resurrection as an event separate from any general resurrection of the dead at the end of time.

It is, of course, one thing to say something "openly" (8:32) and another thing for it to be properly understood. Peter shows his own failure to grasp what Jesus has said "openly" by his reaction: he takes Jesus aside and begins to rebuke him (8:32), because he had not been able to reconcile what Jesus had said would be his fate with his own understanding of what calling Jesus "Christ" had implied. Peter saw Jesus as filled with power and, humanly speaking, never subject to suffering and dying at the hands of other mere mortals. Jesus' countering rebuke says it exactly: Peter is "not committed to the things of God, but to the things of men" (8:33). It is precisely because it is *God's* will that Jesus/the Son of Man "must" die. Peter still has not yet come to see that it is Jesus' own obedience to the will of God which definitively establishes Jesus as righteous and as God's Son, and which gives a perfect example of what true discipleship entails. Peter rather represents what is the normal way of looking at life, that which is focused on the things "of men" but is not "of God."

8:34–9:1   *The Necessity of the Cross and of a Death to Self*

In 8:34–9:1 Jesus uses the misunderstanding of Peter to the prediction of his death *and resurrection* as an occasion for further explaining what is necessary in God's plan for those who would follow Jesus. Denial of self, taking up one's "cross," losing one's "life," letting go of the desire to control one's success, future, etc.: all this is what is required of men and women if they will pass judgment by the Son of Man (8:38). If it was required of the Son of Man himself (8:31), then the disciple who "wants to follow after" him (8:34) should expect no less required of him.

Jesus' saying in 9:1, "Amen, I say to you, there are some standing here who will not taste death until they see the kingdom of God come with power," is capable of being understood in a variety of ways. It seems to take the "future eschatology" of 8:38 and narrow the time of that last judgment down to the lives of those—"the crowd with his disciples" (8:34) —who were in Jesus' audience. In that interpretation, Mark would have certainly felt that he and his reader were living in the last days before the apocalyptic judgment. Perhaps, however, it is a word of *reassurance* after the threat of judgment in 8:38. If the reference to the "kingdom of God come with power" refers not to the eschatological judgment by the Son of Man, but rather to the resurrection of Jesus, then there would certainly be those among that crowd who would experience that event and be brought to see and understand what God requires of humankind; they would recognize in the resurrection of Jesus God's confirming action and would respond in faith, proclaiming among men and women the coming of that new reality, the kingdom of God. And they, like Jesus, would acknowledge the necessity of a life lived not for oneself but for others. Such an interpretation would require that the "kingdom of God" (9:1) is different from and accessible before the coming of the Son of Man (8:38), but that is consistent with other motifs in Mark, e.g. in the parables of chapter 4.

9:2–8 *The Blessedness of Jesus the Son*

Mark indicates a change of scene clearly with both a temporal and a geographical transition in 9:2. The transfiguration of Jesus in 9:2–3, despite its marvelous aspect, is *not* the focus of this story, but really part of the story's setting. The body of this passage is the dialogue between Peter and Jesus and the reproof of the voice from heaven, both of which lead to the climactic focus in 9:8.

The same persons mentioned earlier in 8:28 are found in 9:4. When Jesus had asked "Who do people say that I am?" the alternatives had been John the Baptist, Elijah or one of the prophets. Here in the transfiguration scene, Elijah and Moses (the *greatest* of the prophets) are conversing *with* Jesus; clearly, then, Jesus cannot be identified with either of them and the opinions of people have been refuted in these two cases. Peter then again betrays his failure to understand clearly who Jesus was when he offers to make "three shelters," one for each of the figures; that this is not a response coming from a faith understanding is shown in two ways: Peter and the disciples "were *terrified,*" on the one hand; and the voice from heaven booms out, "*This* is my beloved Son! Listen to *him!*" (9:7), establishing Jesus' clear superiority, on the other hand. Mark then tells his reader that when they looked around, "they no longer saw anyone . . . but only Jesus alone with them . . ." The disciples' model can *only* be *Jesus* and no other.

9:9–13 *Jesus Interprets the Scriptures for the Disciples*

The third alternative of 8:28, i.e. that Jesus might be John the Baptist reincarnated, has not yet been eliminated, but that is taken care of in the episode which immediately follows after 9:2–8, "as they were coming down from the mountain" (9:9). In 9:9–13, Jesus charges his disciples not to tell anyone what they had seen "until the Son of Man had risen from the dead" (9:9). The full sequence of events indicated in the prediction of 8:31

must have run its course before the disciples can tell others what they had "seen"; Mark simply will not show the disciples in a role of full faith, of clear understanding, of openly telling others about *Jesus,* then, because they, in his view, had not progressed to that fullness of faith until after the resurrection. And so, even here, after the transfiguration, his disciples question: "What is 'the rising from the dead'?" (9:10); they incorrectly understand it as a reference to the general resurrection at the end of time and raise the objection, "Why do the scribes say: 'It is necessary for Elijah to come first?' " (9:11). That would be one of the signs that the end-time was approaching. Jesus' answer in 9:12–13 is of interest for two reasons: it agrees that Elijah's "coming first restores all things," but it also suggests that John the Baptist was Elijah, which would eliminate the third alternative opinion from 8:28. The phrase "they did to him whatever they pleased, as it is written of him" (9:13) reminds you of the information given here in Mark's gospel about the death of the Baptist (6:14–29); it implies, moreover, that "the present age has reached its end and the kingdom of God has come near," as Jesus had proclaimed (1:15).

Thus has Mark resolved to some extent the question of Jesus' identity, raised implicitly in 8:21 at the close of his third major section (6:30–8:21) and explicitly in 8:29, at least for three of the disciples: he is *not* the Baptist, nor Elijah, nor one of the prophets. Nor does Jesus want to be called "Messiah," at least for the present. Rather he is privately speaking of himself as the Son of Man, a figure of greater importance than even the Messiah, *and* of his *having* to suffer many things and be killed. That juxtaposition of a figure high on the scale of prestige and authority with a fate at the hands of others, of authority submitting to authority, is signaling to the disciples and to Mark's audience how very different from human wisdom is the wisdom of God.

9:14–15, 16–27, 28–29   A Lesson in True Discipleship

A three part episode now illustrates how the disciple can respond and accept the conditions of true discipleship so strange to our natural judgments. The episode opens with what are, by now, familiar motifs: a large crowd, scribes as antagonists, everyone "utterly amazed" at Jesus (9:14–15).

This transitional phrasing moves the narrative into the passage where "a person from the crowd" addresses Jesus as "Teacher" and explains that Jesus' disciples had been unable to cast a "dumb spirit" out of his son. Jesus' reaction is to lament this generation which has shown itself to be "unbelieving." The disciples were not able to cast out the "spirit" although they had, after all, been empowered to do so in 6:7; their authority is apparently as much limited by the lack of a faith response as was Jesus' in 6:5–6. This generation has also shown itself to be "faithless" in the person of the father in this story, whose desperate request is also lacking in conviction and commitment.

When the boy is brought to Jesus, the enormity of the healing asked for is clear: the boy has been deaf and dumb from childhood, and totally under the power of the spirit (9:21–22). It is no wonder that the father's request is so tentative: "*If* it is possible, help us" (9:23); by every human estimation what is desired is impossible. Jesus' response is almost indignant and certainly a pointed reproof: " 'If it is possible. . . !' *All things are possible to the person who has faith*" (9:23). At this point the story shows the father crying out the words of every true disciple, "I believe! Help my lack of faith!" (9:24). And so the healing can now take place in response to the father's faith.

It is not the miracle which Mark advances for our admiration and wonderment but rather the necessity of a faith which makes all things possible. Even the humanly impossible and unnatural denial of self and taking up on one's cross which Jesus teaches is God's will in 8:27–10:45 *is possible* to the man or woman who "has faith." The father who has been looking for the easy cure, the magical manipulation that would heal his son, had been challenged to "believe." He responds "at once" (9:24) but knows he has only barely moved onto that spectrum of faith responses which will culminate in a full assurance in the power of God operative in God's kingdom; his response shows he senses how close he is still to that natural wisdom and appraisal of things which is "lack of faith." In his prayerful cry, he is a symbol of us all as we confront the challenge to true discipleship.

When Jesus is alone with his disciples (9:28–29), it is clear that they do not understand the lesson of 9:16–27 in the same way. Their concern is that *they* had not been able to "cast it out" despite their previous successes (6:12). Jesus' reply gently nudges them for their own kind of "faithless"-ness; their not having used "prayer" is suggested as a sign that theirs is not yet the confidence that "all things are possible to him who believes" (9:23). The disciples are still far from the true discipleship to which they have been challenged, as will be very clear in the central scene of this concentric structure, 9:30–32, and its follow-up (9:33–37), to which you, dear reader, now turn.

9:30–32   Mid-Point of the Concentric Structure: A Second Resurrection Prediction and the Disciples' Misunderstanding

The central passage in this central section is a scene in which Jesus again predicts his passion, death and resurrection (9:31) to disciples who "did not understand the saying" (9:32) and who "were afraid to ask him." That concise description of the disciples' reaction to Jesus' prediction of his death and resurrection shows clearly that the disciples have not moved beyond their inability to see (8:17), to understand (8:21), and to know (9:6), so that their only appropriate response is to be afraid (9:6). As had occurred before in 8:31–32a, 32b–33, Jesus will go on to elaborate the meaning of the saying in 9:33–37; that further explanation, however, is separated from 9:30–32 by a change of scene in 9:33 ("And they came into Capernaum. And when he was in the house . . ."). The focus of 9:30–32 is accordingly placed both on the climactic assertion of the resurrection in verse 31 and on the fundamental failure of the disciples to understand Jesus' "teaching" (9:31) of what will have to come to pass in verse 32.

Mark tells his reader that the meaning of the passion, death, and resurrection of the Son of Man is one which can only be known by Jesus' disciples; Jesus "did not want anyone to know" where he was because he wanted to teach the disciples privately (9:30). It would be a mistake to see this as an effort by Jesus to keep his own identity secret, as those who propose a "messianic secrecy" motif would assert; rather the secrecy is present because Jesus is trying to bring his disciples to an understanding of "the secret of the kingdom of God" (cf. 4:11), that if one is to come after Jesus, he must deny himself and lose himself (cf. 8:34–35). In the disciples' very human reaction to what Jesus is *insisting* upon by his repetition of the prediction of 8:31, the disciples react *naturally* and without a "faith" response. On a scale of human values and priorities it is natural to assert oneself, to take the initiative and responsibility for making things happen, to "live" life fully so as to thwart the inevitability of death; what Jesus proposes reverses our human and natural wisdom. In their reaction, the disciples represent everyone who has not yet come to an acceptance of the necessity (8:31) of suffering and death even for Jesus, model for all men and women of what God requires.

When in 9:32 Mark reports that "they did not understand the *saying*," the word he chooses for "saying" has the sense of a "declaration," an affirmation of what will come to pass. Only here and at 14:72 does this word occur in Mark. The context for its usage at 14:72 shows that for Mark the word means to convey a sense of a definitive saying about a future event; in 14:72 the definitive declaration had been about Peter's denial, which Peter now remembers; but here in 9:32, that definitive declaration or "saying" concerns Jesus' confident assertion that three days after his death he will rise up. (Parenthetically we can observe that an association of this same Greek word, which we have translated here as "saying" but with the sense of a confident declaration about the resurrection of Jesus, is also made with the resurrection of Jesus in Paul's letter to the Romans 10:8–9; there it is the "saying of faith," the confident declaration "faith" makes—that Jesus is "Lord" and that "God raised him from the dead"—which brings the believer to salvation.)

And so, at the very center of his central section, Mark places a summary of the "secret" God is disclosing through Jesus' teaching and his giving of himself, even to the point of death: *this* is the righteousness which God *will* find pleasing and will reward with continuance beyond death. This is what Jesus had said "openly" in 8:32 and what he is now "teaching his disciples" (9:31). To Mark's reader, this confident declaration of Jesus sends a challenge, not to be like the disciples who "did not understand the saying," but to embrace this righteousness in which one gives oneself in service to others with the assurance that it is the "secret" to entrance into the kingdom of God.

9:33–37 Discipleship Means Giving Up Personal Ambition

The extent to which the disciples misunderstand the meaning of what Jesus has been teaching is illustrated in 9:34: "they had been discussing among themselves . . . 'Who is the greatest?' " Such a concern is appropriate and consistent with our *natural* wisdom which admires success and seeks to measure how much someone has advanced beyond others. But ego-advancement is not what the example of the Son of Man shows the secret of the kingdom to be; in fact a concern with who is "the greatest" is the *very opposite* of a denial of self, a letting-go of self. Jesus responds to this continued lack of comprehension with an example.

Jesus' words in 9:35 are a clear response to the primacy of ego-advancement and self-centeredness implicit in what the disciples had been discussing: "If anyone wants to be first, let him be last of all and servant of everyone." *This* is the meaning of the Son of Man's having to die; there can be no resurrection without that obedient giving up of the self, even to the point of death. And what "must" (8:31) be for the Son of Man "must" be also for the disciple. To enter into the kingdom, to "be first of all," requires that each disciple put the good of the others ahead of his own.

The "of all" phrase makes sense not only in the context of this section on discipleship but also in the context especially of an instruction to "the twelve" (9:35) if it refers to that community of disciples which is the church. Mark does not seem to be a gospel in which the "church" as the community of those who follow Christ is much in evidence; it cannot be, of course, because of the perspective Mark has taken for his story of Jesus. In that perspective, the seeds of the later church/community were sown when Jesus called "those whom he desired" and empowered the twelve; yet Mark cannot write the reality of the "church" which later emerged back into his story of Jesus, because the church, to Mark, is the community of disciples who would "come *after*" Jesus (both in the sense of being a disciple and in a chronological sense: 8:34; cf. 16:7), who will understand what "the rising from the dead" means (9:10) but only after they have had experience of it, and who will after the resurrection proclaim Jesus to be "risen" and "Son of God." Still, Mark's story is not without its clues to the reality of that community life which characterizes the "church," and 9:35 is one of those.

Life in a community requires that each member give up his own self-advancement in the interest of the life of the whole and, hence, in deference to the needs of each other member of the community, no matter how socially and humanly difficult that may be. If the child is an example of the least significant in a human society (the child was without status and privilege in the first century), then the attitude of a true disciple must be such that it can be open even to the "last" in the society that is the church: "receiving" one such child/other member of the community of disciples means putting that one ahead of yourself. To do so is of such critical importance that it establishes a real *identity* between the true disciple and Jesus and, thus also, God (9:37).

And so, Mark has brought us into the heart of the "secret": to be first you must be last; to save yourself you must lose yourself; to have "life" you must "die"—all this in imitation of the model provided for us by Jesus/ Son of Man and in union with him in the community of disciples. Mark, while employing various titles for Jesus—Messiah, Holy One of God, Lord, Son of Man, and preeminently Son of God—has shown that it is important that you "listen to him" (9:8) and be like him. The ethic of *being* "last of all and servant of everyone" will be vindicated, as surely as the resurrection will vindicate Jesus' own suffering and death, by disciples who embrace the ethic of self-denial becoming "first" in the kingdom.

9:38–50   On Being "Salt" and "At Peace with One Another"

That primacy of ethic over a primacy of doctrine or orthodoxy is clearly expressed in the next scene in this section, 9:38–50. There is little disturbance of the setting sketched in 9:33–35a. While a new focus is begun with 9:38: "John said to him . . ." and the subject *seems* to turn to "casting out demons," it really does not. Mark instead shows Jesus exploring yet further the dimension of a community established by an ethic of mutual service.

What bothered John was that "a man" was "casting out demons" in Jesus' name, but was not part of "the twelve" or one of the church community that "was . . . following" the twelve. Jesus' response showed that it is not even nominal church allegiance that is decisive but the doing of that ethic of community-building which is characteristic of the followers of Jesus: "He who is not against us is for us" (9:40). Their support of and generosity towards the church/community (which bears the name of Christ, 9:41) is *like* the disciples' own ethic of mutual service which builds up the community from within. It will, accordingly, not go unrewarded (9:41).

If 9:38–41, then, elaborate the ethic of mutual service characteristic of the community of disciples by acknowledging the value for building up the community even by those who do not "follow" the twelve, 9:42–48 emphasize how much more important it is that no one *within* the community be so "against" (9:40) the essential basis of the community that it prompts others to leave the kingdom of God. This has been an address about community to those within the community: it was to "the twelve," about being the "servant of *everyone,*" about following the twelve, about who is and who is not "for us," and now it concerns "these little ones who believe in me" (9:42). To cause one of them "to sin" is a terrible thing. In a paraphrase consistent with the narrative of this section, then, the saying asserts that "to sin" is to depart from the ethic of mutual service and community up-building; when all the members of the community work together for the good of the whole, community exists because of the power of self-denial and because of the identification with Jesus which that brings into being. When, however, any one member of that community begins to assert himself/herself over against the others, claiming a privilege of ideas or beliefs or status or whatever, that self-advancement is incompatible with what Jesus has taught as the secret of the kingdom of God and tempts others away from the humanly difficult ethic of mutual service characteristic of the kingdom of God. These two competing ways of living are incompatible. The first places you in the kingdom of God; the other is "sin" and moves you out of the kingdom and is to be avoided at all costs: it is better to enter the "life" that is the "kingdom of God" maimed than to be on the outside, whole in body but dead in spirit (9:43–48).

What Jesus is teaching the twelve is summarized in the three "salt" sayings of 9:49–50. There will be a point at which "everyone" will be " 'salted' with fire"; a judgment will inevitably be made on which of the two competing ways of living has been chosen. This first "salt" saying in 9:49, therefore, picks up the theme of 9:43–48. It is also the case that "salt" is unique and that its unique properties of taste and preservation cannot really be substituted for by anything else. "If salt has become tasteless, with what will you season it?" describes the uniqueness of the Christian community that embraces the ethic of self-denial and service of one another; should that community ever abandon the ethic which is "of God," humankind would have lost the unique revelation of the Father's will for men and women which Jesus taught the twelve. The final "salt" saying ties those two ideas of uniqueness and community ethic together: "*You,* have salt *in yourselves* and live in peace with one another." To live in peace with one another *is* to be unique in witnessing to God before the world.

10:1–9   The Crowds Acclaim and the Pharisees Test

The scene changes markedly in 10:1: Mark presents Jesus as no longer "teaching his disciples" (9:31) but as out again in a public ministry, teaching the "crowd" (10:1). What Mark intends his reader to understand is that the content of that teaching was suggested by the very "test" presented to Jesus by the Pharisees (10:2). The case the Pharisees chose concerned the "lawful" character of the practice of divorce according to Moses' revelation of God's law. That the Pharisees fail, again, to know the divine will implicit in the law generally is shown in Jesus' attributing Moses' words permitting divorce to an *anticipation* of the Pharisees' own "hardness of heart" (10:5). Jesus authoritatively proclaims the intention of God to be found in Genesis 2:24 that "the two shall become one," so that "they are no longer two, but rather one body" (10:7–8).

The passage is consistent with the materials which precede it in this section in several ways. First of all, the Pharisees "test" Jesus just as the "scribes" had argued with him in 9:14 (in the corresponding part of this concentric structure). Secondly, a doctrine, even of Moses, is set aside in favor of an ethic that conforms to the purpose which God intended to make known through the law. And, finally, the emphasis on the *unity* established in marriage refracts in its own way the command to "live in peace with one another" in 9:50 and the comments about the very human effort to control one's own life, to "save one's life," which reflects the egocentric drive that leads to *dis*unity. That last emphasis on "unity" anticipates, also, materials which will follow in 10:31 and 10:45.

10:10–12   Jesus Interprets the Scriptures for the Disciples

Mark has often portrayed Jesus as teaching his disciples privately, and the setting for this is once again inside "the house" (cf. 7:17; 9:28). The answer Jesus had given to the Pharisees in 10:5–9 is given again in these verses, but in a clear and unambiguous saying: divorce is prohibited not just for the husband but also for the wife. Mark 10:10–12 function not unlike 7:17–28; a question by the Pharisees and the scribes in 7:5 about observance of a "tradition" had received a response from Jesus which—there (in 7:6–8, 13) more than here, despite 10:5—is a rebuke to the Pharisees, a rebuke citing yet another part of the law in order to correctly interpret the law. Jesus then gives the clear and ambiguous statement privately for the benefit of the disciples.

10:13–16   *The Blessedness of All Who Become Like Children*

The transitional verse Mark provides at 10:13 is an awkward indication of a change of scene because there is no clear antecedent for the "people" who were bringing children to Jesus. Jesus is presumably still "in the house" (10:10) with his disciples, and these "people" would apparently reintroduce the "crowd" of 10:1 in order to provide the sense of a new development.

In this passage the disciples again seem to have missed the essential teaching of Jesus' message, for they "rebuked" those who had brought the children into the private circle around Jesus. After the prediction in 9:31 of Jesus' passion, death, and resurrection, which the disciples had not understood (9:32), Jesus had directly countered the disciples' search for who was the greatest with the succinct paradox that to be first, one must become last and put oneself in a position of service to all others; receiving a child (9:36) had been an example of that paradox which is in its turn vindicated by putting the one who imitates Jesus' action of self-denial into contact with "him who sent me" (9:37). Because of that earlier scene, the rebuke to the crowd (?) by the disciples at the presence of children betrays their continued failure to grasp that fundamental message of the *necessity* of a denial of self in the service of others. The disciples' misunderstanding prompts Jesus' own indignant response (not unlike his rebuke of Peter's rebuke in 8:32–33).

The teaching is again clear here: unless one responds to the kingdom of God "like a child," i.e. in the way Jesus has welcomed (10:14) and embraced the children (10:16), he or she "shall not enter" the kingdom of God (10:15). That new possibility which Jesus initiates is only accessible to those who have made no pretense to power, authority or status but have welcomed, and become like, the child who has none of these. To "such" persons "belongs the kingdom of God" (10:14), and Jesus demonstrates the special favor they enjoy by a three-part symbolic action. He takes these "children" into his arms; he blesses them, and he lays his hands upon them. The imagery of 10:16 suggests a liturgical action which would initiate the true follower of Jesus into full discipleship; as such it not only appropriately rebukes the misunderstanding of the disciples around Jesus in the narrative but anticipates the next passage in 10:17–31.

10:17–31 The Necessity of Giving Up What One Has

The episode Mark places next occurs as Jesus begins to leave the "house" and set out on "a journey." In content it reflects in a number of ways the concerns of its counterpart in the concentric structure, 8:34–9:1. As abruptly as Jesus had begun to talk in that earlier episode (8:34–9:1) about what one must do to "save his life," a man abruptly asks Jesus, "Good Teacher, what must I do to inherit eternal life?" (10:17). In the dialogue which follows it is clear that the man has been a law-observing Jew from his youth (10:19–20). Jesus' immediate response is an emotional one: he "liked him very much" (10:21), seeing in the man someone who was sincerely trying to be righteous before God. There is, however, one thing lacking: the man must give up what he has in material things and then "follow" Jesus (10:21). In that request, Jesus reiterates the requirement of 8:35: "Whoever *loses* his life because of me and because of the good news will save it." The man before Jesus, however, is unable to bring himself to that, "for he had many possessions" (10:22), and Jesus' words in 10:23 indicate that the control which wealth and possessions exercise over a person can make it "difficult . . . to enter into the kingdom of God" (10:23). In that comment to his disciples, Jesus gives focus to the saying in 8:36: "What does it profit a man to gain the whole world only to forfeit his life?"

Since Mark has been presenting the disciples as failing to understand the fundamental teaching Jesus has been presenting, right from the first comment about the necessity of even the Son of Man's having to give himself up to suffering and death, one is not surprised at the reaction of the disciples here (10:24–27). They are "amazed" and "overwhelmed." And in their question "Then who *can* be saved?" Mark's reader can hear, with a perhaps uncomfortable echo of his or her own natural inclination to acquire and to control, the perfectly human priorities we all endorse to some degree. Jesus acknowledges that what is asked here means that we cannot "enter the kingdom of God" and "inherit eternal life" only by our own efforts; it is only "with God" (10:27) that this can become possible.

Just as the passage in 8:34–9:1 had ended with an eschatological warning, so, too, does 10:17–31. In the earlier passage, Jesus' words were an implied threat: failure to respond to *him* and his "*words*" would lead to rejection by the Son of Man (8:38); in 10:29–30 Jesus' words are instead a strong reassurance that those who have left *everything*, even family (!), because of *him* and the good news will receive blessings a hundred times over. Indeed, the point of 10:29–30 is exactly that of 8:35b, right down to the deciding factor; not only must one "lose his life" (8:35b) or have "left everything" (10:28), but it must be for "because of me and because of the good news" (8:35b *and* 10:29).

The closing verse (10:31) cryptically summarizes the point not only of this passage, but also of the whole section (8:27–10:45): that God's will is the reverse of human expectations. It is human and natural to seek wealth and possessions, even to take reassurance in a network of family and friends, to be "first" in the estimation of men; yet that is not enough even if in all other respects one has observed all the commandments from one's youth, like the law-observing Jew in 10:19–20. Jesus does not say that it is impossible for such men and women to inherit eternal life, but that it is "difficult" (10:23) to do so; wealth and possessions can distract from the complete commitment to others of which Jesus had spoken in 9:37, 50 and will reaffirm in 10:43–45. Those who are "first" in human estimation may well find themselves "last," unable to "enter the kingdom of God," as Jesus had threatened in 9:35a, 38; and those who "come after" Jesus (9:34) to "follow" him (9:34 and 10:21), who "have left everything and followed" Jesus (10:28), may have seemed "last" in human estimation but will be judged "first" in the age to come. In one verse, therefore, Jesus has expressed the *wisdom* which is not possible with men but only with God (10:27), which is not of men but of God (cf. 8:33b in the context of 8:31ff).

These two corresponding pieces (8:34–9:1 and 10:17–31), therefore, both describe two contrasting ethics, two opposite views of what is wise, two opposing "wisdoms," and in a fashion not unlike Paul's comments about the "wisdom of the world" and the "wisdom of God" in 1 Corinthians 1. Perhaps these two pieces, or even the entire section, should be subtitled, "The Two Ways," a motif found frequently in Wisdom literature.

10:32–40 A Resurrection Prediction, a Misunderstanding, and a Correction

This passage contains both the third prediction of Jesus' passion, death, and resurrection *and* Jesus' words correcting the fundamental misunderstanding of the disciples; in these respects it corresponds to that first passage where Mark's reader had seen these motifs combined, 8:31–32a, 32b–33.

The transitional verse 32 is either a curiously inept one, or one charged with meaning in its few phrases. What is striking is particularly the detail that "Jesus was going in front of them (the disciples); and they were *amazed,* and those who were following were *afraid.*" Why should the disciples be "amazed" that Jesus was walking ahead of them? That is probably not the focus. Verse 32 had also noted that Jesus was "on the way," going up to Jerusalem," and his walking ahead is a demonstration that he has taken the initiative to go to that death which he had taught (8:31; 9:31) was the "necessary" (8:31) fate of the Son of Man. That the disciples were "amazed" expresses that same failure to understand the divine purpose that necessitated the death of Jesus, a failure which the disciples had shown in earlier episodes in this section (8:27–10:45). That they were "afraid" shows once again how human were their expectations and desires for Jesus and how still limited was their "faith."

Nowhere in the previous predictions had "Jerusalem" actually been explicitly mentioned as the place where the fate of the Son of Man would be accomplished. But Jesus makes it clear in vs. 33: "Look, we are going up to Jerusalem," and this prediction of Jesus' passion, death and resurrection continues in details (10:34) that anticipate those of the passion narrative Mark will present later. The reader now knows that this "good news!" (1:1) about Jesus is approaching the point where the focus must be on the suffering and death of the Son of Man before he "will rise" from the dead.

Just as Peter had demonstrated after the first prediction of the passion that he could not accept or understand the death of the man he had just proclaimed the Messiah by rebuking Jesus, so also is there now a reaction by two other favored disciples, James and John, which betrays their very human but very real misunderstanding of the reason for the suffering and death of the Son of Man. Focusing here on the promise that Jesus would "rise," they ask Jesus if they may sit on either side of him in his "glory" (10:35–37). Just as Peter's rebuke had rejected the teaching of God's will manifest in even the Son of Man's having to give himself over to the control of others, so the disciples' question here shows a failure on their part to acknowledge the necessity of a giving up of "self" which Mark 8:27–10:45 has made so clear.

And just as Jesus had earlier rebuked Peter in the strongest of language (8:33) and referred to what is "of God," so now Jesus responds to the question by James and John that it is not *his* will that would be able to grant such a request (10:40), but "it is for those for whom it has been prepared" (10:40). That means that it is *God* who will grant places of prestige in the afterlife, and Jesus' words about drinking the cup he drinks and being baptized with his baptism, allusions to his own death, indicate further that the positions of prestige will be in accordance with the extent to which a disciple matches the giving up of self for which Jesus is the perfect model.

10:41–45 *What People Do and What the Disciples Must Do*

The contrast between *human* expectations and priorities and the expression of the will of *God* which Jesus is setting for his disciples comes to clear expression in these next verses. In the world, power and authority rule, as is shown in the actions of those who "lord it over" the Gentiles (10:42). Jesus' next words make the contrast very clear: "But it is not to be like that among you!" And the essence of the contrast is this: if there is in the Gentile world acceptance of the primary value of power "among *you*" (and the words are addressed also to Mark's reader!), the primary value must be service to others. "Whoever wants to become great among you shall be your servant; and whoever among you wants to be first shall be the slave of everyone" (10:43–44). And the model for this, as has been clear from the first prediction of Jesus' death and resurrection, is the Son of Man who came "not to be served but to serve, and to give his life as a ransom for many" (10:45). With that verse, this section about the paradox of the first being last and the last being first has found its explicit interpretation: service offered toward others (in community) is what God requires of men and women and is the righteousness which will be rewarded, not the very human quest for power and control over self and over others. This is the wisdom of God which Jesus brings as the righteous and beloved Son of God; this is the "secret" requirement of the kingdom of God.

The "Two Ways" of 8:27–10:45

The contrast which 10:41–45 just made explicit has actually been the theme running through all the materials of this section. It was clear from Jesus' rebuke to Peter in 8:33 that there were two "ways," one "of God" and the other "of men." That motif of "two ways" is one found frequently in the Wisdom literature (cf. e.g. Ps 1:6; Prov 2:13; 4:14, 18), where "way" is used as a summary term for behavior characteristic of one's essential being, either unrighteous or righteous (cf. e.g. Prov 5:21). It is important in the Wisdom literature to know the "way of righteousness," and the figure Wisdom is preeminently the model to be followed: "I [Wisdom] walk in the *way* of righteousness, in the path of justice" (Prov 8:20; cf. Sir 6:26; 14:21, 22).

What comes to expression in 8:27–10:45 especially is what establishes the contrast: a reversal of the human need to assert one's self over against others; the necessity of losing oneself, of leaving everything, of being last of all and servant of everyone, so that to "be first" you must be the "slave of everyone." Mark's reader had heard Mark say that it was Jesus' purpose to preach in the cities (1:38) and had heard many times that Jesus taught the crowds, and sometimes that speaking of the "word" was in the form of parables which they could not understand. Then in the last section (6:30–8:21) Mark's reader saw that Jesus "taught" like Wisdom; *here* is finally heard the *content* of that teaching, preaching, word through which the kingdom of God is accessible.

Perhaps Mark's use of the term "way" in this section is not simply to be understood at the level of a geographical road or journey. It appears in 8:27–10:45 more frequently than in any other part of the gospel (8:27; 9:33, 34; 10:17, 32) and reminds us also of its prominent position at the beginning of the gospel (1:2, 3). The same word, however, is used in the Wisdom literature for patterns of ethical behavior, and at least some of references in this section could be seen as having that sense. When Jesus, accordingly, is "on the way" in 8:27 and 10:32, he is again like Wisdom, walking "in the way of righteousness" (Prov 8:20), obedient to the will of God expressed in the "must" of 8:31. His disciples are those who follow him "on the way" (9:33, 34), even if they do not yet understand what that entails, but can only be "amazed" (10:32). Such a second level of meaning for "on the way" gives added power to Bartimaeus' following of Jesus "on the way" in 10:52, as we shall see. And it also makes clear the irony of the admission by the Pharisees later in 12:14 that Jesus "truly" teaches "the way of God," which is clearly not that "of men."

4′ The Fourth Last Interlude 10:46–52

The Healing of Blind Bartimaeus

Jesus' teaching of the "secret" of the kingdom of God had reached its climax in Mark 10:43–45; indeed, the saying in 10:45, "The Son of Man did not come to be served but to serve, and to give his life . . ." returns to the first passion prediction where Jesus "began to teach them that the Son of Man must suffer. . . ." Mark 8:27–10:45 had presented that teaching of the "secret" of God's will for men and women in two ways: in Jesus' own obedience to the necessity of his taking up his cross and in Jesus' three different ways of amplifying what his action meant for those who would be his disciples.

It was clear from the reactions of misunderstanding described in 8:27–10:45 that the disciples in Mark's narrative are still in a sense "blind" and do not yet "see"; they do not yet understand that discipleship involves recognizing the kind of giving of self which Jesus had taught was the "secret" of the kingdom of God and accepting it. In portraying the disciples in this way, Mark is thoroughly consistent with his conviction that it would not be until the resurrection that the disciples would come to faith and understanding. At this point, the disciples can only wonder, "Then who can be saved?" (10:26), so contrary to human expectations is what Jesus has taught as God's will. Jesus' response is that the kind of giving of self he has taught is necessary *can* be done, but only with God's help: "With men it is impossible, but not with God; for everything is possible with God" (10:27).

It is now that Mark's reader turns to the story of blind Bartimaeus and finds there both an anticipation of Jesus' disciples' coming to full faith (for Bartimaeus personifies full response and true discipleship) and a personal challenge.

There are a number of ways in which the story of the healing of blind Bartimaeus contrasts with the earlier healing of the blind man in 8:22–26. It may not be insignificant, as we shall see, that the blind man is named, for one thing. But then he, on his own initiative, recognizes Jesus, petitions him, eagerly comes to him and *wants to see!* These are all the component elements of the faith response, and in this respect the story of Bartimaeus is so different from the earlier healing of a blind man. In the earlier story (8:22–26), the healing or giving of sight took place gradually, in stages; it is an appropriate parable, therefore, for those disciples like Jesus' own whose faith has not yet brought them to a full acceptance of the necessity of a giving up of self, in imitation of Jesus, the model for all of the will of God for humankind. Bartimaeus, by contrast, is the parable of the kind of disciple Mark would have us all be, whose faith has enabled us to see and to follow on the way. It is not insignificant, then, that Jesus' response is "your faith has saved you," for that "faith" enables the man "to see" that to which he had been blind before.

Coming as it does after Mark's central section (8:27–10:45) in which Jesus has been teaching his disciples about the requirements of true discipleship, the story of the healing of blind Bartimaeus serves as a parable of the true disciple. What Jesus has taught is necessary (8:31), as the will of God for himself and for those who would follow him does not conform to natural, human wisdom which seeks to assert oneself over others; to place oneself at the service of others is not what we would naturally do. And so the response of Bartimaeus to Jesus' question "What do you want me to do for you?" (10:51) is really the response of every person who would be Jesus' disciple: "Master, that I might see!" Born into a blindness that can only embrace human evaluations and priorities, Bartimaeus like every reader and every disciple must be enabled to "see" and accept that God has reversed human expectations.

Perhaps the naming of the blind man is not without some significance. The name "Bartimaeus," like that of his father "Timaeus," is Roman in form, not Jewish. Yet his address to Jesus is that of the faithful Israelite when he calls out "Son of David!" Perhaps here Mark has left a memory of that early Hellenistic Jewish community for whom the traditions of Judaism and the pursuit of "wisdom" were so important and for whom Mark wrote the good news about Jesus. Bartimaeus betrayed a different kind of blindness when he, like Peter (8:29), appealed to Jesus as the Davidic Messiah. What he wants is "to see," just as those in the pursuit of wisdom want "to understand" the will of God so as to become righteous. And he was sitting "at the side of the road," not squarely positioned "on the way," as he will be later. Perhaps these details remember and relate that coming to faith that was characteristic of Mark's own experience and of others in his Hellenistic Jewish, and now Christian, community.

Yet once again Mark has placed a short story about discipleship between major sections of his gospel. Like the other "interludes," it looks backward: to the "blindness" of the disciples, and of all men and women, toward Jesus' teaching of the kingdom of God in 8:27–10:45. And it also looks forward, as Bartimaeus follows Jesus "on the way" taught by Jesus, to Jerusalem and to Jesus' passion and death. To that story Mark now turns.

D' Mark's Third Last Section 11:1–12:40

Jesus Comes to Israel as Its Lord

The healing of blind Bartimaeus in 10:46–52 was a fitting sequel to the section on discipleship (8:27–10:45), as we have seen, but it is also an appropriate bridge to Mark's third last section which begins at 11:1. Bartimaeus had cried out (while still "blind," we should note): "Jesus, Son of David, have pity on me!" That association of Jesus with the kingdom of David will be picked up in the opening scene of chapter 11 when the crowds cry out "Blessed is the kingdom of our father David which is coming!" (11:10). And it will be brought up again at the end of this new development by an enigmatic question of Jesus in 12:37.

Yet the focus of the development in 11:1–12:40 is really not upon the arrival of Jesus as "Messiah." It is instead upon the failure of the religious leaders of the Jews to honor God as they should and to recognize in Jesus the one who teaches what is pleasing to God. We will note later that there are some similarities between this section's emphases and those of the section we think corresponds to it in the concentric organization of the gospel (6:30–8:21). But one should perhaps be noted immediately: when Mark 6:30–8:22 opened, the opening setting was of Jesus and the disciples surrounded by "a huge crowd" (6:34) whom Jesus characterized as "like sheep without a shepherd." In 11:1–10, Jesus enters Jerusalem in the midst of his disciples and a great throng, and in the course of his stay in Jerusalem he encounters those religious groups which *should* have been the "shepherds" of the Jews. Running through the episodes narrated now, however, is the hostility of those religious leaders to Jesus, their failure to acknowledge him, even as "the great throng heard him gladly" (12:37b).

The transitional phrasings which indicate the progress of the narrative in 11:1–12:40 are of interest because of their focus upon both Jerusalem and the temple. Jesus' movements into and out of Jerusalem and the temple are clearly marked, and the temple is the scene both of the prophetic action of a "cleansing" and of a series of encounters with Israel's religious leaders who enter and leave that central stage, as it were. Using those indications of change of scene, the following parts seem to be identifiable:

11:1–11	Jesus enters Jerusalem and the temple, but stays outside
11:12–14	Jesus curses the fig tree in the morning
11:15–19	Jesus cleanses the temple and leaves in the evening
11:20–25	The fig tree is found withered the next morning
11:27	Jesus arrives in Jerusalem and the temple
11:27b–33	priests/elders/scribes question his authority
12:1–12	Jesus gives a parable, threatening them
12:13–17	Some Pharisees and Herodians try to trap him
12:18–27	The Sadducees challenge him, are "very wrong"
12:28–34	A scribe knows God's commandment
12:35–37a	Jesus asks the Son of David question
12:37b–40	Jesus warns against the scribes

If Wisdom motifs influenced the material in 6:30–8:21, suggesting that Jesus had come to Israel as her true teacher, Wisdom, and if those Wisdom influences continued in 8:27–10:45 where Jesus/Wisdom knows what is required both of him and of his disciples by the will of God so that he can distinguish the "two ways," now it would seem that the Wisdom background continues to appear. "Wisdom" had come not just to Israel, but indeed found a dwelling place in Jerusalem (Sir 24:11); Jesus' coming to Jerusalem repeats that motif, but with the emphasis upon Jesus/Wisdom's finding rejection rather than acceptance there.

11:1–11

Ever since the references in 10:32–33 Mark's reader has known that Jerusalem was to be the place of the final rejection of Jesus. And now in 11:1 Jesus and the disciples "came near to Jerusalem" and its environs, most notably Bethany and the Mount of Olives; Bethany will be Jesus' home base until his death, and the Mount of Olives will be the setting for the section following after this one (13:1–37). The references to Jerusalem and Bethany again in vs. 11 close off this opening scene.

The entrance of Jesus into Jerusalem, mounted, riding over a path carpeted with garments and leafy branches, acclaimed by the shouts of

"Hosanna!" from the crowds, has all the marks of the entrance of a royal personage into his kingdom. Indeed, the crowds so acclaim him: "Blessed is he who comes in the name of the Lord! Blessed is the kingdom of our father David which is coming!" (11:9–10). This scene has colored the interpretation of much that follows in Mark's gospel, and seemed to support an interpretation of Jesus as the Davidic Messiah elsewhere in the gospel. Yet it should not be forgotten that not even Jesus' disciples have yet understood the content of Jesus' teaching nor of who he is. The crowds have been constantly "amazed" and "astonished," a sign of their own failure to correctly assess Jesus. Peter's own affirmation of Jesus as the Messiah, moreover, was turned aside in 8:30–33. It is at least possible, therefore, that the crowds here in 11:10–11 remain no more understanding (and no less "blind") than before. Still, Jesus' entrance is a prominent, conspicuous and appropriate one, even if the motif of *mis*understanding prevails and the action is done for the wrong reasons.

Jesus' entrance into Jerusalem is purposeful; his goal is the temple. Every time he enters Jerusalem in the days ahead, he moves quickly into the temple (cf. 11:15; 11:27), the place of his special concern. That detail, too, argues against a too heavy dependence upon an interpretation of Jesus as the Davidic Messiah. The temple setting is not the most appropriate one for suggesting that the new king of the Jews had arrived. But it was the center of Israel's religious practice and a very appropriate place for the clash between the righteousness of God personified in Jesus and the wrong teaching of the religious leaders of Israel.

11:12–14, 15–19

The same movement of Jesus toward Jerusalem, into Jerusalem, and then into the temple occurs again on the second day, but it is broken into two parts, both prophetic; the first anticipates not only the second but also the eschatological completion of the second.

When Jesus leaves Bethany to move toward Jerusalem he encounters a fig tree without fruit. Mark tells his reader that this should have occasioned no surprise because "it was not yet time for figs" (11:13). Yet Jesus "was hungry," and since "he found nothing on it except leaves," he curses the tree: "May no one anymore eat fruit from you ever!" On the literal level the episode seems to show a petulant Jesus throwing a tantrum because he could not get his own way, and no reader of Mark's gospel would be satisfied with that interpretation.

If, however, the scene is viewed as much else in Mark must be, as pointing beyond itself at something else, then the placement of this scene immediately before the scene which follows it suggests an interpretation. When Jesus enters Jerusalem and then the temple, he finds it has been made into "a robbers' cave" (11:17). Those responsible for making Israel a holy people before God had made even the holiest place in Israel unholy, barren, without the "fruit" of righteousness. The fig tree is but a symbol, then, primarily of the temple which Jesus was soon to find defiled, but it is also a symbol of the rejection by Jesus/Wisdom of all that is without the "fruit" which is righteousness before God. Not only does the cursing of the fig tree anticipate the cleansing of the temple, therefore, it also anticipates the destruction of the temple and of all else narrated in Mark 13:1ff. "Wisdom," it should be noted, turns aside from those who turn aside from her (cf. e.g. Prov 1:24–32).

When Jesus enters the temple there is no hesitation: "he began to throw out" those whose activities within the temple were not consistent with its purpose to be "a house of prayer for all peoples" (11:17). Here again the Jesus presented by Mark is one who knows what *ought* to be before God, what the scriptures in fact require (cf. Is 56:7; Jer 7:11). The conflict between the two interpreters of God's will—Jesus and Israel's religious leaders—has been brought to the point of no return, and within the precincts of the temple at that. For now "the chief priests and the scribes . . . were seeking a way to destroy him" (11:18). And the basis for their determination was a fear of Jesus, "for the crowd was overwhelmed at his teaching" (11:18). Those who should have been the "shepherd" of the sheep had to acknowledge that Jesus in his *teaching* the multitudes was providing what they had not.

And once again Jesus leaves the city to reside elsewhere.

11:20–25, 27–12:40

On Jesus' third day, the same movement is observed as on the first two: a movement toward Jerusalem, entrance into Jerusalem, and immediately afterward activity within the temple. And, as on the second day, there is a preliminary episode to Jesus' appearance in the temple, the scene in 11:20–25 where the disciples notice that the fig tree has in fact withered. Because it, like Israel, is now without "fruit," under the curse of Jesus/Wisdom it could no longer live and prosper as do those who respond to Wisdom by doing what Wisdom discloses is pleasing to God. That discovery prompts Peter's amazement and Jesus' cryptic admonition to "Have faith in God!" (11:22). The latter is then expanded a bit awkwardly by a saying about the power of prayer and forgiveness; it is awkward not only because Jesus' words to the fig tree were neither prayer nor done in a spirit of forgiveness but also because the saying is meant to encourage Jesus' disciples; that concern for instructing the disciples, so clear in 8:27–10:45, breaks in upon this narrative's development where the struggle between Jesus and his opponents is emphasized. Indeed, the disciples are with Jesus in the transitional seams, accompanying him therefore along the way of suffering, but they are not otherwise Jesus' principal concern in this section as they had been in the preceding one.

11:27–12:34

On this third day of Jesus' activity in Jerusalem, Mark shows Jesus again in the temple. If on the second day he had cleansed the temple because he had found it wanting so that the "chief priests and the scribes . . . were seeking how to destroy him" (11:18), on this occasion he encounters a series of challenges from those hostile religious leaders and others within the temple precincts.

(11:27–33)

The first challenge in 11:27–33 again puts the "chief priests and scribes" to the forefront, joined by the "elders." Together this group challenges Jesus' *authority* to do "these things"; since they would not have known of the cursing of the fig tree, Mark's reader can only assume that they refer to Jesus' challenge to their own authority in his purging of the temple (11:15–19). Jesus' response is a counter-challenge: he poses a question which the group is unable to answer, because no matter which answer they give, they put themselves in a bad light (11:31–32). It is not insignificant that they have to admit: "We do *not know*," an answer which exposes their real ignorance of the will of God for the Jews. And Jesus' response is to refuse to give them what they sought. After all, by their admission that they did "not know" the source of the authority of the Baptist and of Jesus, the chief priests and the scribes and the elders have acknowledged their own blindness and their inability to see. Rather than come to Jesus/ Wisdom with the faith that seeks to see clearly like Bartimaeus, they came with hostility and a challenge that prevented their ever receiving the blessings which the coming of Jesus could convey.

(12:1–12)

The parable in 12:1–12 is closely connected to what has just occurred. Not only is there a minimal indication of a sequence of events in 12:1 ("And he began to speak to them . . ."), but the "them" can only refer back to the same group that had confronted Jesus in 11:27–33. Mark, moreover, indicates that the same group "knew that he had told this parable against them" (12:12); the parable consequently becomes a continuation of Jesus' rejection of this first group of opponents.

This "parable" is really more of an allegory in that the various parts of the parable can be identified as referring to elements in the history of the Jewish people. The "man" who planted the vineyard is God; the "vineyard" is the Jewish people; the "hedge" put around the vineyard is the law of Moses which defines for the Jewish people the righteousness expected of them by God and at the same time keeps them "holy" and distinct from the neighboring nations. Much depends upon the allusion to "fruit of the vineyard" (12:2). If, as was suggested above, that refers to the righteousness expected of the Jews by God, a knowledge of which was made accessible through the law of Moses, then the identity of the succession of servants becomes clear. The "servant" alludes to each prophet of God who came along in the history of the Jewish people exhorting them to repentance and reform, to become a "holy" people before their God. The "farmers," therefore, would be the religious leaders of the Jews who have prevented the Jewish people from achieving that holiness by blocking the efforts of each prophet: they "sent him away empty-handed" (12:3); "treated (him) with no respect" (12:4); "beat" and "killed" others (12:5). Finally, the "beloved son" (12:6) can only be a reference to Jesus; the group Jesus is addressing would not have understood that reference, but Mark's reader certainly would not have misunderstood it after the baptism and transfiguration episodes read earlier.

The difference in the treatment of the "beloved son" should not be overlooked. The "farmers" "took him" and "killed him," but they had done the same to earlier "servants" sent by the owner of the vineyard/ God. No, Mark adds as the crowning insult that "they threw him out of the vineyard" (12:8). That word, "threw out," had been used a great deal before in the gospel, usually in association with the casting out of demons by Jesus or his disciples, and so it carries with it the overtone of complete rejection. Here the direction of the complete rejection is reversed: the "tenants"/religious leaders complete their ignominy of killing the "beloved son"/Jesus/Wisdom by "throwing him out"/rejecting him completely and by excluding him from the "vineyard," i.e. from inclusion in the people of Israel. The emphatic placement of this phrase at the end of verse 8 completes the picture of Israel's religious leaders' total rejection of Jesus/Wisdom, therefore.

Jesus' rhetorical question in 12:9 about the response of the "owner of the vineyard"/God leads into a threat against the "farmers" (who will be destroyed) and the "vineyard" (which will be given over to others). The theme of reversal which Mark had put forward earlier ("the first shall be last . . .") is sounded again here. The scripture citation in 12:10 gives the other side of the theme of reversal when the citation remembers that "a stone which the builders rejected, this has become a cornerstone" (and thus "the last shall be first . . ."—10:31). The threat is not missed by the opponents of Jesus, "for they knew that he told the parable against them" (12:12) and they "left him and went away," a phrasing which has almost as ominous a tone as the comment in 11:18 that they "were seeking how to destroy him."

(12:13–17)

The second scene (12:13–17) portraying opposition to Jesus while he is within the temple precincts names two different parties, the Pharisees and the Herodians whose purpose is no less hostile than that of the chief priests, scribes and elders: they sought "to find a mistake in what he was teaching" (12:13). Even though they address Jesus as "Teacher" and say that "we know that you are honest . . . [and] in truth teach the way of God" (12:14), Mark quickly notes their "hypocrisy" (12:15).

The "trap" they lay before Jesus is a now-famous dilemma: "Is it permissible to give a poll-tax to Caesar, or not?" (12:14). They thought that Jesus in opting for one or the other interpretation of what was "lawful" would be offending some significant group. To say it was "lawful" to pay taxes to Caesar would offend many Jews who found the posturing of the emperor as a divine being blasphemous; and to say it was *not* lawful to pay taxes to Caesar would put Jesus in hot water with the Romans who would see his response as seditious.

Jesus' first response is to ask his questioners for a coin, "and they brought one" (12:16), a detail that would also be a partial self-indictment of them because it was a tacit acceptance of Caesar's authority over them. A careful, law-observant Jew might have sought to avoid the coin with its likeness of the Caesar who made himself like God; yet these Pharisees and Herodians *know* whose likeness and inscription was on the coin (12:16). Jesus' final response then moves beyond the debate of what is "permissible" according to an interpretation of the law of Moses. In his saying, "The things which belong to Caesar, give to Caesar; but the things which belong to God, give to God!" (12:17), Jesus' words are an authoritative judgment that separates what is "of God" from what is "of men," a contrast which Mark had emphasized earlier in his gospel. What God requires is the giving up of self in the service of others; what Caesar requires is the payment of taxes and the acknowledgement of Roman authority in matters that have little to do with how we become the servants of one another. That would be particularly true if the focus were upon the kind of *self-restraint* which makes true Christian community possible. In any event, Jesus' response is given not on the authority of the Jewish law and tradition but on his own authority. When Mark notes, "and they were utterly amazed at him" (12:17), he once again reminds his reader that Jesus "was teaching them like one who has authority, and not the way the scribes taught" (1:22), a motif encountered early in this gospel.

(12:18–27)

Then a *third* religious group, the Sadducees, comes forward with yet another challenge (12:18–27) centering on the correct interpretation of the law of Moses (12:19) and the belief in resurrection. The Sadducees "say that there isn't a resurrection" (12:19) and pose a question which in simply human terms would make the idea of resurrection ridiculous: if a woman had been wife to seven men, "in the resurrection to which of them will she be a wife?" Since Mark's gospel had shown Jesus three times predicting the resurrection of the Son of Man/himself (8:31; 9:31; 10:33), Jesus' response is predictably an immediate rejection of the Sadducees' position: "You are wrong" (12:24; repeated in 12:27). And, as has been implied before, the fundamental source of the error of the Sadducees is that they "know neither the scriptures nor the power of God" (12:24); they have misinterpreted a particular passage "in the book of Moses" (12:26).

When God said to Moses, long after the death of Abraham, Isaac, and Jacob, "I am the God of Abraham, and the God of Isaac, and the God of Jacob," God showed that he was God not "of the dead, but of the living" (12:27). Once again Jesus shows his ability to penetrate to the meaning hidden in the text of the law of Moses and to reveal it with authority.

(12:28–34)

The final scene (12:28–34) in this grouping of challenges (11:27–12:34) posed to Jesus by the religious leaders of the Jews appears at first glance to be yet another hostile effort to put Jesus on the spot. Still, the transitional phrases which introduce this episode suggest that the challenge is not really so hostile. The question asked of Jesus is offered not by the scribes as a group, but by only "one" of them, who had seen that Jesus had "responded to them well" (12:28). The test seems to be offered by this one scribe as an effort to confirm his approval of Jesus.

The scribe confronts Jesus with yet another controversy within Judaism: "Which commandment is the most important of all?" (12:29). And Jesus' answer again transcends that debate about one commandment being "first" and transforms it. The commandment to love God "with all your heart, and with all your soul, and with all your mind, and with all your strength" recalls Deuteronomy 6:5; but the explanation of that is made specific: "You shall love your neighbor like yourself" (12:31). The second transforms the first from a piety that could lapse into mere formal ritual into an ethic that must guide the ethical behavior of all men and women toward one another. When the scribe approves that interpretation of the commandment to love God in terms of loving one's neighbor as oneself, he draws out precisely that implication: "to love the neighbor like oneself is far better than all the whole burnt offerings and sacrifices," a reference perhaps to 1 Samuel 15:22.

Jesus' observation that the scribe with that attitude was "not far from the kingdom of God" (12:34) brings this episode to a climax. After all, there is little difference between Jesus' insistence that one must give up of oneself to save oneself, that one must become the servant of all, and the statement that one must love one's neighbor as one loves one's own being. To do *that* requires esteeming one's neighbor as no less of value than oneself and, perhaps, even preferring his well-being ahead of one's own. In this is the love of God, the first of all commandments, actually realized. An ethic of service has been placed before an ethic of formal worship, which can be sometimes empty and lacking in the personal effort.

12:35–37, 38–40

At this point, Mark seems to indicate that Jesus has turned away from the religious leaders who had been challenging his authority and teaching in the temple. While the setting is still the temple (12:35), it is now the "large crowd" which "listened to him eagerly" (12:37b). In 12:38 the reference to Jesus as "teaching," already mentioned in 12:35, is repeated; since the setting remains unchanged, that repeated reference to teaching in 12:38 seems to create a double scene. In its first part, Jesus disputes a specific point of scribal teaching; in the second, Jesus warns against the scribes because of their behavior.

The first part of the double scene seems at first glance to develop a curious point: "How can the scribes say: 'The Christ is the Son of David'?" (12:35). From our vantage point in the tradition, that association of the Christ/Messiah with the son of David seems a given certitude; and yet here Jesus is contesting it! The essence of Jesus' argument is that the "Messiah" must be something more than just the "Son of David." The basis for the argument is the supposition that David wrote the verse of Psalm 110:1 cited in Mark 12:36 and so spoke of the Messiah as "*my* Lord," implying a recognition of the Messiah's superiority over David, and so also over any son fathered by David.

There is in Mark a certain ambiguity about calling Jesus the Messiah. On the one hand it is an appropriate designation, as in 1:1, "The beginning of the gospel of Jesus *Christ.*" And yet it is always in some way inadequate as a full designation of the identity of Jesus; even in 1:1 it is immediately qualified by "the Son of God." When Peter acclaims Jesus as the Messiah in 8:29, Jesus responds by forbidding the disciples to say anything more about that and corrects Peter's misguided concept of Jesus' role in the verses immediately following (8:30–33). When Bartimaeus calls Jesus "Son of David" he does so while "blind," and it is only when he acknowledges Jesus as "Master" (10:51) that his personal "faith" in Jesus allows him to see and to follow Jesus "on the way" to Jerusalem and the taking up of the cross. And when Jesus is about to enter Jerusalem he speaks of himself not as the Messiah, but as the "Lord" who has need of the colt (11:3). He is acclaimed by the crowds as "he who comes in the name of the

Lord" (11:9), and they quickly associate that with the "kingdom of our father David" (11:10); and yet for all that, the "multitude was overwhelmed at his *teaching*" (11:18).

And so, too, here does Mark seem bent upon dissuading his reader from a too easy identification of Jesus as the mere Messiah. Again, the Messiah who is the Son of David is to be distinguished from the Messiah who is something more than that, who is the "Lord." Later in chapter 15 it will again be seen that the identification of Jesus as "the Christ, the King of Israel" (15:32) receives its correction in the mouth of the centurion: "Surely this was the Son of God!" (15:39). These shifts of emphasis throughout the gospel challenge Mark's reader to move beyond the label "Messiah" or "Son of David" in its usually accepted sense and to understand that element of superiority which makes Jesus "Lord," even David's "Lord." The "way" of God described in 8:27–10:45 which Jesus acknowledges and then teaches his disciples, i.e. the giving up of self in the service to others and in obedience to the will of God, is precisely what makes Jesus more than simply the Son of David, who like David would rule over a kingdom of subjects. Jesus has come to Israel, to Jerusalem, and to the very temple as the one who "in truth" teaches "the way of God" (12:14), as the "Teacher" (12:14; 12:19; 12:32) who teaches "in truth" what is the essential commandment of God (12:32). It is for *this* reason that Jesus is appropriately called "Lord," not because Jesus realizes the traditional hope for a king (it is probably not coincidental that Peter calls him "Rabbi," or "my Lord," in this section, 11:21). After all, from the perspective of Jesus' teaching, the "Messiah" who is David's "Lord" would place himself at the service of his subjects (10:42–45).

In the second part of this episode, Jesus attacks the behavior of the scribes themselves, a behavior which is consistent with their understanding of the Messiah as a "King" who rules, and just as mistaken as was Peter's in 8:32–33. If the scribes thought that the Messiah was a "King" who would rule, they also seemed to think that they could adopt behavior affecting personal superiority over others. They like Peter and the disciples in 8:27–10:45 do not recognize that the will of God requires an attitude of service, that the "love of neighbor" must be like loving oneself (12:33), sometimes putting the good of another first. The warning is clear: that attitude illustrated by the scribes "will receive the more severe condemnation" (12:40). After all, it was their responsibility to preserve and present the law of Moses to others; *they* should most certainly have known what it taught. Since their responsibility was greater, so too will their "condemnation" be greater.

And so in this double scene there has been a subtle return to elements of the opening account of Jesus' entrance into Jerusalem. If in 11:1–11 Jesus who is the "Lord" is popularly acclaimed as the one bringing the kingdom of David and then goes into the temple, here in 12:35–37 Jesus is in the temple, listened to by a great throng, and teaching that the Messiah/Son of David is not really the "Lord." And if 11:12–19, the cursing of the fig tree and the cleansing of the temple, are critiques of the ethical understanding and behavior of the religious leaders, and particularly of the "chief priests and the scribes" (11:18), here in 12:38–40 the scribes' hypocritical attitude is warned against and threatened with "the greater condemnation."

These observations suggest that Mark 11:1–12:40 is organized in the following manner: a double scene opens and closes the section (11:1–11, 12–19; 12:35–37, 38–40); the major part of the section is the series of arguments between Jesus and the religious leaders of the Jews (11:27–12:27) about "knowing" the scripture and what is "of God"; bracketing that central episode and separating it from the opening and closing scenes are episodes where Jesus defines elements of discipleship in the kingdom of God (11:20–25; 12:28–34).

a. 11:1–11 Jesus is acclaimed as "Lord" and Davidic Messiah
  b. 11:12–19 Jesus curses a tree without fruit, symbol of a barren temple; priests and *scribes* seek to destroy him
    c. 11:20–25 Jesus, with his disciples, talks about "faith"
      d. 11:27–12:27 Jesus debates religious leaders of Jews about scripture and about what is "of God" or "of men" (11:30; 12:17)
    c′ 12:28–34 Jesus, with one "not far from the kingdom," talks about the most important commandment
  b′ 12:35–37 Jesus distinguishes "the Lord" from "Christ"/Son of David
a′ 12:38–40 Jesus warns that the *scribes* will be condemned for their hypocrisy.

In 11:1–12:40, therefore, Mark has brought the "way" which is "of God" into a face-off with the way which is "of men." Jesus who is Wisdom, who in his teaching feeds the shepherdless people far more abundantly than the law of Moses could do (6:30–8:21), who knows what the law of

Moses meant to disclose as God's will (7:1–23; cf. 12:13–34), and who teaches what is the "secret" of the kingdom of God (8:27–10:45), now comes to the very center of Israel to confront those whose responsibility it was to shepherd Israel. One after another those religious leaders are shown to "not know" (11:33) what is "from heaven" and are silenced (12:34) by the "true teacher" of God's way. What God requires is righteousness as Jesus has disclosed it, a giving of self in service to others. Just as the fig tree was cursed and withered because it bore no fruit, so too will these "farmers" or cultivators of God's "vineyard" Israel find that the vineyard will be given to others (12:9). There will be a "condemnation" (12:40).

Observations About the Gospel's Concentric Structure

Mark 11:1–12:40 is positioned in the concentric structure of Mark's gospel so as to correspond to 6:30–8:21. There are a number of ways in which these two sections are alike.

1. In both sections, Jesus is on a journey and many respond to him.
2. In 6:34 Jesus found the people "like sheep without a shepherd"; in 11:17 he finds the temple turned into a "robbers' cave."
3. In both sections, the central position is given to a confrontation between Jesus and religious leaders (7:1–23; 11:27–12:27), over matters of the law and its correct interpretation; and in both Jesus is shown to know what is the intention of God.
4. In both sections there is a "nature miracle" after the opening episode (6:45–52; 11:12–14).
5. In each there is a specific challenge to Jesus. In 6:30–8:21 the Pharisees seek a "sign" from heaven to confirm Jesus for them (8:11), which Jesus refuses to give (8:12); in 11:1–12:40, the chief priests and scribes and elders seek to learn "with what authority" Jesus acts (11:28), and Jesus refuses to tell them (11:33).
6. Both sections end with a warning: 6:30–8:21 with a warning against the "leaven" or teaching of the Pharisees and the Herodians (8:15), 11:1–12:40 with a warning against the scribes (12:38–40).
7. In both sections the portrayal of Jesus emphasizes elements from the story about the Wisdom of God. In 6:30–8:21 the emphasis is on Jesus' coming to Israel to teach what men and women need to know

is pleasing to God, feeding them with "the bread of understanding" and penetrating to the intention of the law. In 11:1–12:40 the emphasis is on Jesus' coming to Wisdom's own place, Jerusalem, as in Sirach 24:10–11, and teaching. Indeed, in Sirach 24:11 it is precisely in Jerusalem that Wisdom has her "authority," the focus of the challenge to Jesus in 11:28.

These observations of similarity between 6:30–8:21 and 11:1–12:40 confirm their being corresponding sections in the overall concentric structure of Mark's gospel.

3′ The Third Last Interlude 12:41–44

The Widow Who Gives All She Has

There can be little question Mark intended this scene to be closely associated with the preceding verses; its central character is a "poor widow" (12:42), reminding Mark's reader of Jesus' condemnation of the scribes because they "devour the estates of widows" (12:40) and in their hypocrisy think that their long prayers can be pleasing to God. Moreover, Mark situates this episode still in the temple precincts; not until 13:1 does the scene significantly change when Jesus *leaves* the temple.

The contrast in 12:38–40 had been between those who position themselves ahead of or above others and those vulnerable persons in our society who are easy prey because they, like the widows, have no persons of status to defend them. As we saw, those verses came to their climax with a threat against the hypocritical and rapacious (12:40).

When Mark turns to the story in 12:41–44 he presents a slightly different contrast and an entirely different climax. The contrast is ostensibly between the rich people who "contributed a great deal" of money into the treasury (12:41) and the widow who "gave two small copper coins (which is one fourth of a cent" (12:42). The rich are not criticized, however, as were the hypocritical scribes; rather the "poor widow" is praised because "she in her poverty gave everything she had, her whole existence" (12:44). One misses the emphasis if this is seen as a contrast between two economic groups, with the impoverished in some way favored. The poor widow is praised because of the *way* she gave what she had; she gave *everything* she had. Here again is heard Jesus' insistence that the giving of self must be complete; it is no accident that Jesus' words about the necessity of losing oneself in order to save oneself (8:34–9:1) had been paralleled in the concentric structure of 8:27–10:45 by the words of Jesus to the rich young man (10:17–31): "Go, sell whatever you have and give to the poor" (10:21). Here in 12:41–44 that insistence on a complete giving of oneself is shown by the example of the "poor widow" and is praised.

114

As a reminder of Jesus' fundamental teaching and as an anticipation of the narrative of Jesus' death (chs. 14–15), this particular vignette is not in any way an anti-climax but the strong restatement of what Mark presents Jesus' fundamental principle to be and for which God himself affirms Jesus to be his "Son."

Like all the other "interludes," therefore, Mark 12:41–44 looks backward: to the mention of "widows" (12:40) and to the ethic of a giving of self (8:27–10:45). It also looks forward: to Jesus' own giving of everything he had, his very life. And it presents, once again, an example of true discipleship.

Observations About the Gospel's Concentric Structure

In several places we have observed that Mark has placed short episodes or "interludes" which illustrate as narrative parables the fundamental lesson of his gospel for those who would be Jesus' disciples: it is God's will that we place ourselves totally in the service of our neighbor, for in doing so we also love God (12:39–41). The central section of Mark's gospel (8:27–10:45) was preceded and followed by vignettes about the healing of blind men/disciples (8:22–26; 10:46–52). The sections preceding (6:30–8:21) and following (11:1–12:40) that material shared a number of elements in common, as we have just seen. Now it is apparent that Mark has positioned the passage about the widow who gave everything she had (12:41–44) so as to correspond in the concentric structure of the gospel to the story about John the Baptist who gave everything *he* had, his very life (6:14–29). These two episodes graphically illustrate for the disciple what the commitment to the teaching of Jesus requires: a *complete* giving of oneself according to the circumstances of one's personal life. This is what is required of the disciple who wants to follow the example of the righteous Son of God who "did not come to be served, but to serve and to give his life" (10:45).

C′ Mark's Second Last Section 13:1–37

Of Discipleship and Judgment

In one respect the story of the widow's gift has broken the tension which had been building in Mark 11:1–12:40. That section had ended with the warning, "Watch out!" (12:38), the same phrasing which recurs in 13:5, 9, 23 and 33. And that warning had in turn looked ahead to the "more severe *condemnation*" (12:40) of the scribes for their hypocritical behavior. The description of the end of the world and its judgment would have followed naturally enough from this material. So, too, would the change of scene in 13:1, because Jesus had been "in the temple" since 11:27, as 12:35 indicates, and the indication that "he was coming out of the temple" in 13:1 ends that presence. Consequently the reference to the treasury in 12:4a seems determined by the story of the widow's gift, and both appear to intrude upon an originally clearly developing narrative leading to the eschatological discourse in chapter 13.

Yet the story of the widow's gift in 12:41–44 has also made the transition to the introduction of Jesus' apocalyptic discourse in Mark 13:1–37 an easy one. That discourse is prompted by the admiration of the disciples at the beauty of the Jerusalem temple complex, an admiration which was well deserved because of the temple's monumental size and white marble facade. Yet the story of the widow had had as one of its lessons the moral that one must not judge by appearances; "rich" and "poor" are contrasted in 12:42–43, and "abundance" and "poverty" in 12:44, with the lesson taught that riches and abundance are as nothing if they are not given totally and wholly to God. So, when the disciples admiringly marvel, "What stones and what buildings!" (13:1), Jesus' reaction is entirely consistent: despite their beauty, "there will not be left here a stone upon a stone which will not be pulled down" (13:2). To ask whether this is a prediction of or reflects knowledge about the actual destruction of Jerusa-

116

lem and the temple complex by the Roman army in 70 A.D. is to obscure the lesson. Beauty, like riches and abundance, can be an empty and ultimately foolish vanity if the way one lives is not a sure preparation for God's final judgment. A beautiful temple cannot by itself make a people holy; they must do that themselves, as the "cleansing of the temple" episode in 11:15–17 had shown and as the warnings to "take care" and "watch" in 13:1–37 underscore.

That Jesus is referring to God's final judgment is not lost on the disciples who in 13:4 ask for information on *when* "all these things" are to be "accomplished" and on the *signs* which will precede it. The question artificially sets up the development in 13:5–37 which proceeds in reverse order: the "signs" are presented in 13:5–23 and the time "when" the apocalypse of the Son of Man will occur, in 13:24–37.

The evangelist has once again made his reader privy to a "private" (13:3) conversation between Jesus the "Teacher" (13:1) and his closest disciples. When the discourse begins with the words "Take care that no one leads *you* astray" (13:5), Mark's reader cannot but hear these words of Jesus as addressed personally and directly, such was the skill of Mark's presentation to include the reader as part of the audience with Peter and James and John and Andrew.

Perhaps it would be best to call attention here to the two kinds of material one finds in 13:5–37. There are phrasings which are in the second person and directly addressed to an audience (13:5–7, 9–11, 13a, 14a, 18, 21, 23, 28–29, and 33 to the end); and there are phrasings which are in the third person and constitute a narrated discourse (13:8, 12, 14b–17, 19–20, 22, 24–27, 30–32). Mark appears to have had traditional materials available to him in those phrasings which are in the third person. They are markedly apocalyptic in character and, if read consecutively, have a coherence of their own. It is hard to imagine that Mark would have chosen to borrow apocalyptic material from Jewish materials when the authoritative voice for him was that of Jesus; perhaps in these third-person phrasings we can hear an echo of the apocalyptic challenge of Jesus himself. There is in these phrasings a vocabulary which is not found elsewhere in Mark; for example, "false christs" and "false prophets" and the verb "to lead astray" used in 13:22 are only found in this verse, and the references to the "elect" occur only here in 13:20, 22, and 27.

Read consecutively, these third-person phrasings have a distinctive rhythm and a power. Moreover, a characteristic fourfold juxtaposition of images occurs in 13:8, 12, 15–16, 24 and 27, and its effect is to leave an audience with the sense of a *full* description of what has not been fully described at all but only broadly sketched.

A table of "signs" in this third-person, traditional layer of materials is described. There would first be a period of sufferings (8) in which the fabric of the political order is torn apart as nations rise against nations and the natural order is similarly in upheaval from earthquakes and famines (8). Even the strongest of bonds would be ripped apart as members of families turn against each other (12). This "affliction" (19; 24) will last for a period of time, referred to ambiguously as "those days" (17; 19; 24), and a sure sign of that period will be the appearance of "false Christs and false prophets "to lead astray, if possible, the elect" (22). And then as the *final* "sign" the order of the cosmos itself will be thrown into disorder: "the sun will be darkened, and the moon will not give its light, and the stars will be falling from the sky, and the powers in the heavens will be shaken" (24–25). And then the Son of Man will appear in splendor for judgment (26–27).

Following this table of signs is material that voices an ignorance of exactly *when* the end will occur. However strong the confidence that there will be a vindication of the "elect" in an apocalyptic period culminating in the appearance of the Son of Man, the refusal to claim a knowledge about when it will occur is just as strong (32). And yet, if the exact *hour* may not be known, at least it is believed that it will be soon, for there is the assurance that "*this generation* will not pass until all these things happen" (30). How should we understand "this generation"? In the original complex of materials we are reviewing, it certainly meant that the coming of the Son of Man in judgment would happen during the lifetime of the hearers of Jesus. At the time Mark employed these materials, some of "this generation" would probably have still been alive but nearing the end of their lives. Yet for the evangelist and his reader, this apocalyptic warning seems not to have had quite the same immediacy, as a review of the other layer materials—the Markan redaction—shows.

Before Mark makes use of the first of the "signs" in 13:8, i.e. that "nation will rise up against nation," he makes the comment that "when you hear of wars and rumors of wars, do not be alarmed; it is not yet the end" (7). It was an unsettled political world in the Israel of the late 60s of the first century; before the decade would end, Roman troops would besiege Jerusalem. Mark's comment seems to acknowledge that turmoil but at the same time to discount it as being the beginning of the "end." What is necessary is to "endure to the end" (13). And that act of enduring will be one of witnessing to Jesus and to the gospel (9–10); the expression "because of me" (=Jesus) has appeared twice before (8:35; 10:29), and both times it is also associated with the "good news!" or gospel. In vss. 9–10, therefore, Mark seems to have added yet another criterion for discerning when the end will really occur: "To all the nations must the good news first be preached." That the evangelization of the entire world has not yet taken place is the fundamental reason why the "it is not yet the end" and why the faithful disciple must "endure to the end."

In view of this sense of a somewhat more remote and delayed coming of the Son of Man, one can understand the motif with which Mark unifies the traditional layer of material and his own comments: the caution to "Take care!" in verses 5, 9, 23 and 33. The apocalyptic warnings remain valid because they will inevitably come to pass. But in the meantime what is necessary is rather to be careful not to be deceived and misled and to remain faithful disciples. The picture in verses 9 and 13 is a grim one: "they will deliver you [disciples] up to councils; and you will be beaten in synagogues . . . and you will be hated by everybody because of my name." In the face of such hardship, some might find other interpretations of discipleship attractive, particularly if they did not call one to the necessity of taking up one's cross as Mark's gospel so clearly has done; such interpretations of what being a disciple of Jesus entails might even be done in the name of Jesus (5, 21), but their effect would be really to "lead astray" the disciples (5). Mark's cautionary "Take care!" accordingly envisions an extended period of delay before the coming of the Son of Man and during which remaining faithful in discipleship is not easy.

In his redactional modifications, therefore, Mark is continuing his description of true discipleship and of response to Jesus who has come to Israel to "teach" the way of God. Between this moment when Mark's reader hears Jesus' warnings about the final end and the coming of the Son of Man, and its actual occurrence, what is necessary is to remain vigilant and loyal, steadfast even in the face of harassment, and a witness to Jesus and the gospel before all men (9–10). The coming of the Son of Man will be the definitive vindication of the elect, of those to whom the secret of the kingdom of God has been "given" (4:11) and who "hear the 'word' and embrace it and bear fruit" (4:20). But that "time" cannot be anticipated (33), and so one should be watchful (33, 37), alert and not "asleep" (36).

Observations About the Gospel's Concentric Structure

It should not be overlooked that Mark's redactional touches have taken the original apocalyptic material and refocused it into an appeal to the disciples to remain faithful in their response to Jesus. In that respect Mark 13:1–37 resembles 3:20–6:13 where the materials principally speak of diverse responses to Jesus' own preaching and a future judgment is referred to as a vindication for the faithful response to Jesus; apocalyptic is placed at the service of an exhortation to discipleship, much the way it was in Mark 4:24 where the same "Take care!" motif is found in an eschatological context.

Because the apocalyptic emphasis has been reduced and the focus is on discipleship, the materials in 13:1–37 do not awkwardly interrupt the story line developing from 8:31 on, and especially from 11:1 on, i.e. about the death of Jesus. Mark's recasting of the apocalyptic materials into a private address to Peter, James and John (13:3) has become, rather, the reiteration of the necessity of the disciples' taking up of their own cross and for their carrying on in their lives the ministry of Jesus. During Jesus' lifetime, theirs had been a ministry of preaching and casting out demons (6:7–13); after his death it will become a ministry of witnessing "to them" and of remaining faithful even when *delivered up* and persecuted. The Markan redactional touches suggest that something of what is described in 13:9–10 has been indeed the experience of his own community.

When Mark's reader began the materials the evangelist had gathered together in 3:20–6:13, one of the first scenes met was one in which the proper response to Jesus was the key element (3:21–30); even then rumblings of a future, divinely initiated sorting out of the responses to Jesus could be heard in 3:28–29: "All things will be forgiven men and women, sins and blasphemies whatever the blasphemies may be; but whoever should blaspheme against the Holy Spirit will *not ever* have forgiveness, but is guilty of an *eternal* sin." Response to Jesus' teaching and resistance to the overtures of Satan would be the key, as the parable of the sower, its explanation and 4:12 indicated. The intimation of a future judgment was again clear in 4:22–25: "For a thing is not hidden except for the purpose of its being made manifest, nor is a thing made secret but that it should become clear.... Understand (='Take care!') what you hear! With the measure you use to measure will it be measured out to you and provided for you. For he who has, it will be given to him; and he who has not, even what he has will be taken from him." Moreover, the images of the "sickle" and the "harvest" in 4:29 and the admonition to the twelve to "shake off the dust . . . as a witness against them" in 6:11 continued to present a promise of a future and final separation of men on the basis of their response to Jesus and his teaching. Here in 13:1–37, Mark's second last section which corresponds to his second major section (3:20–6:13) in his concentric plan for his gospel, the evangelist gives a fuller description of the what, when, and how of that *final* "end."

Besides the elaboration in 13:1–37 of these intimations of judgment in 3:20–6:13 just noted, there are other correspondences of wording and of phrasing.

We have noted before Mark's use of the verb "to see" as a metaphor for "to understand" (8:18; cf. 4:12). The verb actually occurs fourteen times in Mark. Eight of those instances are *in the same form* as the verb we translate here as "take care!" (4:24; 8:15, 18; 12:38; 13:5, 9, 23, 33); it is always addressed to the disciples and is used as a warning in all those cases except 8:18. Clearly this is an element of Markan redaction. What is of particular interest is that the warnings to "take care!" in chapter 13 elaborate the first of those warnings in 4:24, which is in the context of an eschatological warning, as we noted above.

If Mark's extended use of "take care" reminds the reader of that first warning in 4:24, another striking correspondence with Mark 3:20–6:13 is found in 13:9. When the disciples are delivered up to councils and beaten in synagogues, it will be to be "a witness to them" (13:9). That *same* commission had been given to the healed leper in 1:44, but it was conspicuously the climactic charge to the disciples themselves *in 6:11!*

Finally, there is one other observation. It surely can be no coincidence that there are only three usages of the word "end" in Mark (3:26; 13:7, 13). The first of these is at 3:26: "Satan . . . is finished," coming to an end; in its context, the parable speaks of that end of Satan's reign as something which is *not* happening: since Jesus is not casting out demons by the power of Satan (3:22), Satan's house is not divided (3:26) and so is not coming to an end. But it is clear from 3:27 that Jesus in casting out demons is the one who "*first* binds the strong man" [Satan] so that he "*then* plunders his house." The "end" of Satan's house is implied in 3:27; the references in 13:7 and 13 insist that the disciple must endure until that "end" is accomplished (13:3).

2' The Second Last Interlude 14:1–9

Of Jesus' Departure

Jesus' teaching about the "end" came to an abrupt halt in 13:37. The unity of the discourse in chapter 13 had been clearly established by the summarizing question the disciples ask in 13:4 and by the repetition of the "take care" warning. Nonetheless there is an awkwardness here which is uncharacteristic of the Markan editing of his materials, in that no transitional phrasing blends the material of 13:1–37 into the story of Jesus' passion which follows it. From those dire warnings of chapter 13 Mark's reader is moved quickly into the announcements of 14:1–2 without learning what had happened to Jesus and the disciples. Since the material in 14:10–15:39 is a structured and coherent unit, as we shall see, these verses in 14:1–9 stand apart. They are yet another example of Mark's placement of episodes which speak in various ways of discipleship between major sections of his gospel.

The story of the woman's "anointing" of Jesus with a costly ointment, the disciples' reaction to that and Jesus' gentle reproof of them embodies yet another lesson on discipleship for the reader to hear. In the indignation of the disciples at the waste of this precious and valuable ointment one hears again the indignation of Peter after Jesus' first passion prediction; there, as here, the fundamental misunderstanding is an effort to grasp and hold onto what is valuable and precious in our eyes. It is a truism in our society that "we put our money where our mouth is," and we indicate what we think is of worth by what we will pay the most for. Money, now as in this story, can be a sign for what we value and want to hold onto. Sometimes the misunderstanding can even be prompted and justified by laudable motives, as it is here when the disciples want to sell the ointment in order to have money to give to the poor. But lying behind those motives is a hidden conviction that *we* should *control* the future and determine the outcome of things. Discipleship is, rather, the acknowledgment that it is necessary to give of oneself and to let go and relinquish even

122

that very human need to be in charge of our own futures. There is a fundamental acceptance of God's will which comes to expression in this story; the woman's attitude contrasts with that of the disciples who still fail to understand Jesus' teaching of God's wisdom for humankind and who would shape and mold and influence the future by capitalizing on the monetary worth of the perfume. Her attitude is instead focused on what the will of God requires in the present moment: "What she was able to do, she did" (14:8), and in this she has become an apt paradigm of true discipleship. And in that attitude of acceptance of God's will, she also anticipates the perfect illustration of the acceptance of God's will which Jesus will make in Gethsemane and on the cross, thus confirming that he is, indeed, the Son of God.

Jesus, who has tried to teach the disciples ever since 8:31 that what is necessary is to conform to the will of God for each of us, now must teach them once again to leave aside considerations that are "of men" and human and turn to the fundamental reality of his own death; his comment that the disciples will not always "have" Jesus (14:7) is a reference to his death, and the anointing, he says, is in anticipation of his own burial (14:8).

And so, this episode, like the others, looks backward and forward and speaks of discipleship. It looks backward to that early intimation of his death in 3:6 and to the scenes of popular acclaim for Jesus when he entered Jerusalem in 11:1–10, 18 and 12:37b. It looks forward to the unfolding of the story of Jesus' passion and death in 14:10–15:39 and to the story of Jesus' burial in 15:40–47. The woman's gift to Jesus is a sign of her acceptance of that story as God's will for Jesus and also for herself; as all disciples must, she has recognized the necessity of giving oneself and what one has. Jesus' promise that "wherever the good news is preached throughout the world, what this woman has done will also be spoken of in memory of her" (14:9) is an affirmation that in what the woman has done one can find an object lesson on true discipleship.

Observations About the Gospel's Concentric Structure

Since Mark has organized his gospel into a concentric pattern, it is not surprising that there should be a number of ways in which this interlude, despite its different content, reflects elements of that corresponding interlude in 3:7–19. That earlier passage had followed immediately upon the conspiracy of the Pharisees and the Herodians against Jesus, their intent being to destroy him (3:6); this passage begins with the blunt statement that the "chief priests and scribes were seeking how to arrest him by stealth, and kill him" (14:1). Here, as there, the passage falls into two parts, 14:1–2 and 14:3–9. And again as in 3:7–19, the first of those two parts presents Jesus as surrounded by a crowd; it is implicitly present in the hesitation of the chief priests and scribes to kill Jesus "during the feast, lest there be a tumult of the people" (14:2). Moreover, and again as in 3:7–19, the second of those two parts presents Jesus as alone "with" his disciples; although the episode speaks of his anointing by a woman who remains present throughout the story (see verses 5 and 6), the concern is about Jesus not being with the disciples always (verse 7). If in the earlier interlude Jesus had called the twelve "that they might be *with him*" (3:14), now Jesus clearly announces that the disciples will not always "have" him (14:7). That remark and the reference to Jesus' burial move the reader smoothly into the narrative of Jesus' passion which immediately follows.

B' Mark's Last Major Section 14:10–15:39

The Betrayal, Rejection, and Death of Jesus

The preceding interlude (14:1–9) had hinted that Jesus' story might end in his death; that is, after all, clearly the intention of the chief priests and scribes in 14:1, and Jesus himself seems to acknowledge its nearness with his words in 14:7–8. And now, Mark's reader must confront the apparent tragedy of Jesus' betrayal, rejection and death. There have been numerous times since 3:6 when the reader has been forewarned that Jesus' story will not, in human terms, have a happy ending: he whom the reader has known to be the Son of God "must," as Jesus himself insisted in 8:31, "suffer many things and be rejected by the elders and chief priests and by the scribes and be killed." Yet the "tragedy" is only apparent, for always there is the assurance that after three days he will "rise again." Before that vindication can occur, however, it is necessary for Jesus and for those who follow him—including Mark's reader—to experience the agony and pain of a rejection by one's own, a rejection so total that it refuses to Jesus even a right to life, and this from a people who greatly value life as a gift from God.

The material in 14:10–15:39 amplifies the three fundamental phases of the first passion/resurrection prediction in 8:31. When the details of all three passion/resurrection predictions are set side by side and compared, they combine to summarize the three phases of the passion of Jesus narrated in 14:10–52, 14:53–15:1, and 15:2–39:

Passion Predictions
and the Markan Passion Narrative

Passion Narrative	8:31	9:31	10:33–44
14:10–52	"Son of Man" (2×) "must" "suffer many things"	"Son of Man" "will be" "delivered" (paradidomi)	"Son of Man" "will be" "delivered" to chief priests and scribes
14:53–15:1 (inclusion unifies)	"be rejected by the elders and chief priests and scribes"	"into the hands of men"	"they will condemn him to death" "and deliver him to Gentiles"
15:2–39		15:16–20	"they will mock him" "spit upon him" "scourge him"
	"be killed" "rise"	"be killed" "rise"	"kill him" "rise"

Each of the three parts of the story of Jesus' passion, moreover, is a clearly organized and distinctive whole, and each has a thematic emphasis as a result of the way in which the materials are organized. Mark's reader will see Jesus betrayed, rejected and denied (even by his own!) and crucified as the "King of Israel" (when he was "truly the Son of God").

A. Mark 14:10–52   Jesus Is Betrayed

The parts of this section of Mark's passion narrative are clearly indicated by the changes of scene in 14:10, 12, 17, 22, 26, 32, and 43. The opening scene in 14:10–11 speaks of "Judas" as "one of the twelve," of his offer to "betray" Jesus, and of the "chief priests"; all of these references appear also in 14:43–52, the scene in which the actual betrayal is narrated. Mark 14:10–11 and 14:43–52 bracket these materials, and the following organization of the parts of this section is suggested:

a) 14:10–11
Judas offers to *betray* Jesus to the *chief priests*

b) 14:12–16
time frame reference: first day of unleavened bread
the disciples go to the city
preparations for the Passover/last supper meal
an upper room is "ready"
Jesus is accepting of whatever has been prepared

c) 14:17–21
time frame reference: evening
Jesus comes with the twelve to table
and speaks of being *betrayed*

d) 14:22–25
bread/body—blood/cup poured out

c′) 14:26–31
Jesus goes with the twelve to the Mount of Olives
and speaks of being *denied*

b′) 14:32–42
they go to Gethsemane;
preparations for "the hour" (of betrayal/doing
Father's will), vs. 41;
Jesus is ready to do the Father's will
and goes to be betrayed

a′) 14:43–52

the betrayal is complete:
Judas the "*betrayer*" gives the sign (vss. 44–46) to the
crowd, including the "*chief priests*" (vs. 43)
The scriptures are fulfilled (vs. 49)
all forsake Jesus (vs. 50); cf. 14:27

The Betrayal of Jesus

The motif of 14:10–52 is clearly announced in its opening verses: "betrayal." It is Judas' intention in 14:10 and 14:11, and a reference to "betrayal" will occur frequently here (14:10, 11, 18, 21, 41, 42, 44); indeed, it will occur in four of the seven parts of this block of material. (Note that the English translation obscures the correlation above of this block of material to the second and third passion/resurrection predictions in Mark's central section; although the Greek verb is the same in these verses as it is in 9:31 and 10:33, there the translation chosen was "delivered up." The pertinent Greek of 9:31 and 14:41, however, provides identical phrasings.)

14:10–11

These verses concisely anticipate the content of 14:10–52: Judas and the chief priests are set over against Jesus, to "betray" Jesus. Mark underscores the apparent tragedy of this conspiracy by reminding his reader that Judas was "one of the twelve." The first reference to Judas had occurred in 3:19 when Mark lists the names of the twelve; these were those whom Jesus had himself chosen and called (3:13). That Jesus had wanted Judas to be part of the twelve and had called him "to be with him" (3:14) suggests that Mark understands this betrayal as also part of the divine plan which will "require" (8:31) that the Son of Man "must" suffer many things. The betrayal by one of Jesus' own, while by human understanding a "tragedy," will be reversed, however, by God's own action vindicating Jesus—the resurrection.

Judas is mentioned only three times in Mark. In 3:19 Judas' name ends the list of the twelve with the ominous designation attached to it, "who also betrayed him," anticipating 14:10. Since Judas is named again only at 14:43, the verse which opens the last scene of 14:10–52, it would seem that Mark has used the references to Judas in 14:10 and 43 deliberately to frame the narrative of Jesus' "betrayal" or "handing over" to the "chief priests."

14:12–16

With this next scene in the narrative of Jesus' betrayal, Mark underscores again that Jesus' death is a necessary part of the divine plan for Jesus. That the scene occurs "on the first day of the feast of Unleavened Bread, when they sacrifice the Passover lamb" (14:12), provides a setting in which to interpret Jesus' own role; unlike the Passover lamb which is led passively to its sacrifice, *Jesus begins* the series of events which will lead to his death. Here again he is accepting of and obedient to the will of the Father for him. He tells his disciples to "go into the city" and to "follow" a man carrying a jug of water and, "wherever he enters" (14:14), to request a room from the householder there. The *"wherever"* is significant: it matters not where it happens to be, for Jesus is obedient to whatever the Father wills. That this is the emphasis Mark intends his reader should perceive is again made clear in 14:15 when Jesus tells his disciples that the householder will show them "a large upstairs room *set and ready*"; all has been prepared and the divine plan must unfold to its end. Even the conclusion to this scene echoes the emphasis, for the disciples "found it just as he had told them" (14:16).

14:17-21

If 14:12-16 had spoken of Jesus, 14:17-21 speaks primarily of the disciples. In the context of eating at table with the twelve (14:17-18), Jesus speaks of betrayal by "one . . . who is eating with me" (18), who is "dipping in the dish with me" (20). Mark's reader knows that Jesus speaks of Judas. But Judas is never named in Mark (compare Mt 26:25) and so the focus remains upon the reaction of the disciples, who ask "one after another, 'It's not me, is it?' " (14:19). The very anonymity of the disciple who would betray Jesus makes that question one every follower of Jesus must ask. Judas' betrayal has become paradigmatic of those who would later compromise their commitment to Jesus for "money" (14:11) or for some other reason.

Only if this scene is read as a lesson to all disciples generally does the ending verse make the most sense. Verse 21 speaks again of the necessity of Jesus, the Son of Man, having to die according to the divine plan: "for the Son of Man goes as it is written of him," an echo of 8:31. But the threat in 14:21b-c seems odd. If Jesus had to die in obedience to the Father's plan, Judas' betrayal must also have been a part of that plan; is Judas then cursed because he was complying with God's plan for Jesus? That warning makes more sense, however, in the context of a scene about discipleship generally, than about Judas in particular, for once a disciple has chosen to follow Jesus, that commitment has ultimate consequences. Immediately after the first passion/resurrection prediction, Jesus had said: "Whoever is ashamed of me and of my words . . . the Son of Man will also be ashamed of him, when he comes in the glory of his Father with the holy angels" (8:38). The warning in 14:21b-c—"Woe to that man through whom the Son of Man is betrayed! Better for that man if he had not been born!"—reiterates the full commitment that discipleship entails and the either-or quality it imposes.

14:22-25

The central scene in this narrative about Jesus' betrayal is, appropriately, the description of Jesus' actions over the bread and the cup. The actions of Jesus with each are spoken of in parallel: he took . . . he blessed/

gave thanks . . . he gave it to them; and each is then made identical to Jesus: "this is my body" (14:22); "this is my blood" (14:24). The scene captures the essential structure of what Jesus' followers have celebrated as the eucharist, the meal of table fellowship when Jesus is experienced as present among his disciples.

To focus on that eucharistic allusion, however, is to miss the emphasis Mark has given to this scene by its placement and by its content. In 14:12–16 the emphasis had been upon the will of the Father for Jesus and Jesus' obedience to it; in 14:17–21 the emphasis had been upon the disciples as they were warned against repeating the betrayal of Judas, but the death of Jesus is still in focus in 14:21a. Here in 14:22–25 Jesus symbolically gives of himself as he will later give of himself on the cross. Both the bread which is Jesus' body and the cup which is Jesus' blood are *given* to the *disciples;* in the parallel descriptions of what Jesus does with each, the final, emphatic act is the *giving* of each to the disciples as a gift of Jesus himself. Mark has shown Jesus as understanding that what God requires of him is to give *himself* to his disciples, totally; the physical act of accepting his crucifixion is the demonstration that the giving of himself to his disciples is total; he is, indeed, like the blood of the covenant, poured out "for many" (14:24).

We have suggested before that ideas run parallel between this section (14:10ff) and 8:31ff. One more may be seen in Jesus' death as the total giving of himself. That idea had been expressed in another lesson to the disciples in 8:35: "Whoever wants to save his life will lose it; and whoever loses his life . . . will save it."

If the giving of the bread and cup symbolizes Jesus' giving of himself on the cross, then the focus of 14:25 becomes clear. When Jesus says, "Amen I say to you, no longer will I ever drink of the fruit of the vine until that day when I drink it new in the kingdom of God," it is a proclamation of his assurance that he, the obedient beloved Son, will "rise again." The "day" on which Jesus will drink the cup again is the resurrection, the event that will establish the kingdom of God in power and actuality. Jesus' oath is the assertion of his confidence that the Father will not let death prevail over his righteous Son, and in this we hear an echo of Wisdom 2:22–3:9. And, once more, we hear also an echo of the materials in Mark 8:31ff. Jesus' words to his disciples there had ended with a similar assurance: "Amen I say to you, there are some standing here who will not taste death until they see the kingdom of God come in power" (9:1), a reference to Jesus' resurrection.

14:26–31

This scene parallels 14:17–21 in the concentric structure Mark gave the narrative of Jesus' "betrayal" (14:10–52). In that earlier episode, Jesus had predicted betrayal by one of his own and had warned against *any* disciples betraying the Son of Man. In this scene, Jesus says to the twelve (presumably: they have accompanied Jesus since 14:17), "*All* of you will be scandalized" (14:27). Jesus words in 14:30–31 make it clear that this being scandalized means *denying* him. In 14:17–21, the disciples ask uncertainly "It's not me, is it?" Here Peter vehemently insists, "If it's necessary for me to die with you, I will *never* deny you" (14:31). Just as the earlier episode had made Judas' betrayal a lesson about discipleship, so does this episode make Peter's affirmation of total commitment to Jesus a lesson about discipleship. What Peter affirms is what all disciples affirm: "And they all said the same" (14:31b).

Jesus' citation of Zechariah 13:7 in Mark 14:27 is sobering: at the death of the shepherd, the sheep who follow him will be scattered. And when confronted with the necessity of giving oneself to the point of death, disciples who follow Jesus will find it *humanly* impossible to do so. Jesus' resurrection, however, reverses human expectations. If in 14:21 the "Son of Man *goes* as it is written concerning him" to his death, in 14:28 Jesus says, "After my being raised up, I will *go* before you to Galilee." The resurrection is the coming of the kingdom of God in power, reassuring and enabling the disciples to give totally of themselves, as Jesus had. Until the resurrection, however, followers like Peter may well "be scandalized" and "be scattered."

14:32–42

When the scene changes to Gethsemane, the focus is again upon Jesus, as it had been in 14:12–16. There Jesus had accepted *whatever* the Father's will might require of him; here in 14:32–42 Jesus confronts the reality of what the Father requires. The "hour" of his betrayal (cf. 14:41) is at hand, and Jesus is "utterly dismayed" and "much distressed" (14:33) by what it will cost him. When the moment to make a decision or ratify a choice arrives, one cannot rely upon even one's closest friends. Jesus leaves Peter, James and John and goes apart "a little" (14:35) to be alone with the Father and to pray that, "if possible, the hour might pass from him" (14:35). Founded upon the confidence that "everything is possible" to God (14:36) so that even his will for Jesus could be changed, Jesus prays, but his prayer remains that of one accepting of and obedient to the Father's will: "Not what I will, but what you will . . . " (14:36).

Jesus had asked his disciples to "watch," to "stay awake" and alert (14:34). When Jesus returns and finds them sleeping (14:37), he poignantly makes his own experience a lesson for the disciples: "While the spirit is willing, the flesh is weak" (14:38). Having voiced this human frailty, he again goes apart from the others and prays, "saying the same thing" (14:39), i.e. "not what I will, but what you will." When Jesus returns after this second time of prayer, he again finds the disciples sleeping. What words were exchanged, Mark's reader can only imagine; for Mark says only that the disciples "did not know how to answer him" (14:40), leaving the responsibility for Jesus' obedience to the Father entirely with him.

Mark similarly does not say anything specific about Jesus' third period of prayer, but only that Jesus returned a "third" time (14:41) to find his disciples sleeping. There is a sense of finality and completeness to the number three; Jesus had said that Peter would deny him three times (14:30), and he does (14:71). There had been three passion/resurrection predictions. Now Jesus has at least twice asked the Father that he change his plan for him; if the third period of prayer was like the first two, then Jesus had learned through his three petitions that God's will for him would *not* be changed. And so when he returns to the disciples the third time he speaks with acceptance and obedience: "Enough! The hour has come. Behold, the Son of Man is betrayed into the hands of sinners" (14:41).

And just as in 14:12–16 Jesus had taken the initiative to begin the sequence of events which would lead to his death, so too does he here. He rouses the disciples to meet the irrevocable moment of betrayal: "Get up! Let's go! Behold, he who betrays me approaches" (14:42).

14:43–52

The narrative of Jesus' betrayal which began in 14:10 comes to its conclusion in these verses. "Judas" is reintroduced, together with a "crowd" sent by the "chief priests" and the scribes and the elders (14:43). Mark's reader is told in 14:44 what the act of betrayal will be—a "kiss" of greeting. But the word which Judas speaks is unanticipated: "Rabbi!" Is this address of Jesus as Judas' "master" irony? or hypocrisy? or habit? or real affection? Mark does not tell us, but he has underscored yet once again that Jesus' betrayal is by one of his own!

There are two other events which Mark narrates as part of this scene. In 14:47–50 there is an incongruous episode; "one of those present drew his sword" and cut off the ear of a servant of the high priest (14:47). The point of 14:48 is to suggest that it was one of the *armed crowd* (cf. 14:43) sent to capture Jesus that had then turned on the servant of the high priest, and not one of Jesus' own disciples. Matthew and Luke in their gospels recognize this second difficulty and make it clear that it was one of Jesus' own who had tried to defend Jesus (Mt 26:51; Lk 22:49–50); that enables those evangelists to emphasize the freedom with which Jesus accepts his betrayal (see Mt 26:52–54; Lk 22:51). But Mark has his own succinct way of expressing Jesus' acceptance: "Let the scriptures be fulfilled!" (14:49), and the awkward introduction of 14:47–48 can in no way distract from that climactic saying.

There remains only the reporting of the fulfillment of Jesus' words in 14:27: "and *everyone* abandoned him and fled" (14:50). "A certain young man" followed along with him for a while, but when he, too, was "seized," he also "fled" (14:52). Jesus goes to meet the events which bring his story to an end with only Mark's reader still there to hear and see them all.

B. Mark 14:53–15:1 Jesus Is Rejected by All

14:53–54

In order to show that Jesus is rejected by all in Mark 14:53–15:1, Mark will describe two scenes. In 14:55–65 Jesus will be "judged . . . deserving of death" (14:64) by the various leaders representing the Jewish people; and in 14:66–72 Jesus will be "denied" by Peter, representative figure for Jesus' own, the disciples. These verses in 14:53–54 both provide a transition from the narrative of Jesus' betrayal and also introduce the principal actors in the two scenes of rejection in 14:55–65 and 66–72. With the repeated reference to the "chief priests, with the elders and scribes" in

15:1, these verses also fulfill a bracketing function, establishing 14:53–15:1 as a distinct part of the Markan passion narrative.

14:55–65

After the transitional verses of 14:53–54 which set the stage for Jesus' rejection by everyone, there is a new beginning made at 14:55 with the phrase: "But the chief priests and the whole sanhedrin were looking for evidence against Jesus in order to put him to death, and they could not find any." The last part of that phrasing is amplified by the material in verses 56–59 about the witnesses whose testimony was "false" and "did not agree," noted in the beginning and ending comments (14:56 and 59).

A new development occurs in 14:60–64 centering on the high priest and his questioning of Jesus. At first the high priest is an apparently sympathetic judge, asking Jesus for his "answer" to the testimony against him. "Yet he was silent and did not answer anything." What *could* Jesus say that would alter the course of events which would bring to realization the Father's will for him? But there is a question Jesus can answer. When the high priest asks "Are you the Christ, the Son of the Blessed One?" Jesus affirms his identity unambiguously: "I am."

Two things should not be missed here. First of all, the question is not about Jesus' identity as the Messiah. Not only does the addition of "Son of the Blessed One" qualify Jesus' being called "the Christ," but the high priest reacts as though Jesus had blasphemed, a reaction hardly likely if the high priest had understood Jesus to identify himself principally as "the Christ." No, the reaction is surely to Jesus' affirming his identity as the "Son of the Blessed." The second thing to notice is Jesus' next words: "And you will see the Son of man sitting at the right hand of the Almighty and coming with the clouds of heaven." Jesus once again proclaims his confidence that there will be an event in which his identity will be vindicated on a cosmic scale. The language and imagery is that of traditional Jewish apocalyptic expectations, and we are reminded of 8:38 and 13:26–27. But what should not be missed is that Jesus uses it to speak of his being approved by the judgment of God brought by the Son of Man. Jesus is God's Son in his full obedience to the Father's will for him, in a righteousness that will be publicly acknowledged. The high priest's judgment of blasphemy and the whole council's condemnation of Jesus to death are signs of their refusal to acknowledge Jesus' true identity; theirs will be the fate described in 8:38.

Jesus has been rejected by the leaders of the Jews; his rejection is compounded by his humiliation at the hands of the guards in 14:65.

14:66–72

The scene changes in 14:66 to the courtyard below and to different events. The principal figure is Peter who three times is challenged to identify himself as *"with* the Nazarene, Jesus" (14:67) and he would not. After Peter's very explicit third denial, "I do not know this man of whom you speak" (14:71), a cock's crow sounded again and Peter remembered what Jesus had said of him in 14:30.

Even Peter, representative of the disciples and sometimes their spokesman, had fallen away and rejected Jesus. To his credit he immediately acknowledges his failure to live up to his boastful promises of 14:29 and 31 by throwing himself down and weeping (14:72). Still, when the narrative of Jesus' passion resumes in 15:1 in the "morning," Jesus is alone, rejected by even his own.

15:1

This verse with its return to the role of "the chief priests . . . with the elders and scribes" marks the end of this amplification of the second part of the predictions of Jesus' passion, that Jesus be rejected by all. We have seen his rejection by "the elders and chief priests and scribes" of which 8:31 spoke and his condemnation to death foretold in 10:33. What remains is the one thing this verse supplies: "and they bound Jesus in chains and led him away and handed him over to Pilate." With that detail, the prediction of 10:33 that they will "hand him over to the Gentiles" has come to pass. With that phrasing, too, does the Markan passion narrative move to its third and final stage.

C. Mark 15:2–39   Jesus: "King" and "Son of God"

The first part of Mark's passion narrative, about Jesus' betrayal by Judas (14:10–52), fell easily into a concentric pattern. So too does this third and final part.

    a) 15:2–5
        Jesus before Pilate: "King of
        the Jews"?
        b) 15:6–15
           crowds, urged on by the chief priests,
             reject Jesus as "King of the Jews"

           c) 15:16–20
             Mocked by Roman soldiers as "King of
             the Jews"

Death
of Jesus,   d) 15:21–27
"King of the Jews"   Jesus crucified as "King of the Jews"
and   c′) 15:29–32
"Son of God"
           Mocked by chief priests and scribes as "King
           of the Jews" and by other Jews

    b′) 15:33–38
        Death of Jesus < rejection of Jews
        (Temple veil is torn in two)

a′) 15:39
    Centurion (= contrast with Pilate): truly
    "Son of God"

The above shows the prominence of the "King of the Jews" title given to Jesus in this part of the passion narrative; it appears in every episode except the last two. Yet as we have observed before in 1:1, 8:29–30 and 14:61–62, the affirmation of Jesus as the "Christ" or the "King" of the Jews is not correct unless it is qualified by the designation "Son of God." The centurion will give expression to that correction in 15:39. Jesus by his death on the cross gave everything he had, his very life, in obedience to the Father's will and in doing so demonstrated to all that he was truly God's obedient and beloved Son.

15:2–5

After the transitional verse in 15:1 this opening scene of the narrative of Jesus' death can begin immediately, for Pilate has already been introduced. The question Pilate asks Jesus again concerns his identity: "Are you *the King of the Jews?*" By its position at the *beginning* of this development in 15:2–39, it becomes the question put before the reader also, and it controls the presentation of these episodes, as we shall see. It is clearly a formal title, because it begins with the definite article and appears that way in all its subsequent usages in 15:9, 12, 18, 26, and 32. This formal title has not appeared previously in Mark's gospel; and so Pilate's question explicitly raises the question of Jesus' identity as "the Christ" of which the reader has had some awareness since the opening verse of the gospel. When Jesus had asked his disciples at the beginning of Mark's central section (8:27–10:45), "Who do people say that I am?" (8:27), Peter had given what was for him the definitive answer, "You are the Christ!" (8:29). Jesus' reaction there was one which avoided accepting that identification (8:30). Then, later in 12:35–37a, Jesus had himself raised the question of the identity of "the Christ." Peter's affirmation that Jesus was "the Christ," the anointed one, the one who would be the King of the Jews, and Jesus' puzzling attitude toward that title, had remained undeveloped until now.

Jesus' answer here is more informative by its lack of affirmation than by anything else. When the high priest had asked, "Are you the Christ, the Son of the Blessed One?" (14:61), Jesus' response had been unambiguous: "I am" (14:62). When "the Christ" was qualified by "Son of [God]," Jesus can acknowledge it. Here, however, Jesus' reaction is, in effect, a shrug of the shoulders, a dismissal of the allegation: "You have said so" (15:2). The formal title invoking a claim to the political role and power of "the Christ" as "the King of the Jews" was not of interest to Jesus because it was unqualified by the title "Son of God," signifying radical obedience to the will of the Father.

In 15:3 the pattern of 14:55–61 is repeated: "The chief priests accused him of many things." Pilate (as the high priest had done before him) asked in the very same words: "Are you not going to answer anything?" And Jesus, as before, was silent.

The scene ends with Pilate's reaction: Pilate "wondered." Caught up in the unfolding drama of God's will for Jesus, Pilate finds it impossible to understand in human terms; for the easiest answer an accused man could make to Pilate's question would be "No," and the consequences of the seditious claim could be avoided. Even a "yes" answer would be intelligible, for there were many claiming fanatically to be the fulfillment of Jewish hopes for a strong political leader. But Jesus' silence suggests even to Pilate that something beyond the normal and the human was happening, and he could only "wonder" what that might be.

15:6–15

An intensification of Jesus' rejection by his own people occurs in these verses. The introductory verses in 15:6–8a explain that Pilate has an option; he can offer to free Jesus under the custom of an annual pardon of one prisoner. Perceiving that the personal motivation of the chief priests is "*envy*" (15:10), Pilate seeks to avoid their influence by an appeal to the crowd and suggests that he release for them "*the King of the Jews*" (15:9). The chief priests intervene and prompt the crowd to ask for the release of the murderer, Barabbas. And so Pilate puts the fate of Jesus directly in the hands of the crowd: "What then [do you want] me to do with [the one called] *the King of the Jews*?" (15:12). Their response is chilling: "Crucify him!" In two words, the crowd, representative of all the Jews of Israel, had rejected the man presented to them as their "King," the man whom as recently as 11:9 they had acclaimed with hosannas, the one who had come to Israel to teach it the way of God because he was graced with the Wisdom of God.

Pilate affirms his own judgment of Jesus' innocence in his question to the crowd, "Why? What evil thing has he done?" (15:14), but it is a futile effort; the crowd cannot be dissuaded. So Pilate releases Barabbas and hands Jesus over to the soldiers to be scourged prior to his crucifixion.

Twice Jesus was presented to his own people of Israel as their "king" and twice they had rejected him, even when confronted with his fundamental righteousness. It is as though they were made incapable of any other response. The words of Wisdom 2:21–22, 24 seem best to describe what is happening here:

> ... they were led astray,
> for their wickedness blinded them,
> and they did not know the secret purposes of God,
> nor hope for the wages of holiness,
> nor discern the prize for blameless souls;
> ... but through the devil's *envy* death entered the world.

Is it only coincidence that the fundamental motivation of the chief priests is perceived to be "envy"? That word occurs nowhere else in Mark. It occurs only four times in the entire Old Testament, two of which are in the book of Wisdom. One text is that cited above in Wisdom 2:24; the other is in Wisdom 6:23 and is equally suggestive: "... envy does not associate with wisdom." What is coming to pass is the radical choice between the wisdom which is of God, found in Jesus, and the "envy" which is "of men" and blinding them, driving them into unrighteousness.

15:16–20

There is no other way to describe what takes place in these verses than to use Mark's own summary: the soldiers "ridiculed" Jesus. Condemned to death as the "King of the Jews," Jesus is now the sport of the "whole battalion" (15:16) of soldiers; those Gentile soldiers give Jesus the purple cloak of royalty and a crown and they salute him: "Hail *King of the Jews*" (15:18) and kneel in homage to him. What makes this clearly a *mockery* is that the crown is of thorns, and that the soldiers strike his head and even spit upon him.

There is not a word about Jesus' reaction to these actions by the soldiers. He has not spoken since his non-response to Pilate in 15:2. Jesus had spoken of this part of his task in the passion/resurrection prediction of 10:34: "They will mock him (the same verb as in 15:20!) and spit upon him and scourge him." And so Mark's reader is not surprised by this brutal mocking of Jesus. Still, Jesus' *silent* suffering is remarkable; what comes to mind is again a passage from the book of Wisdom where the ungodly men reveal their plans for the righteous man who is God's Son (Wis 2:18):

> Let us test him with insult and torture,
> that we may find out how gentle he is,
> and make trial of his forbearance.
> Let us condemn him to a shameful death . . .   (Wis 2:19–20a).

When the soldiers have finished their play, they strip Jesus of the symbol of royalty, the purple cloak, and put his own clothes on him. And then they lead him out to crucify him, a "shameful death," indeed.

15:21–27

Mark has placed the account of Jesus' crucifixion in the center of the concentric structure with which these episodes are arranged. Even in English translation the sparseness of this account is clear: eight statements in seven verses, and all but one (15:25) beginning in Greek with the simplest of conjunctions, "and."

21 And they pressed into service a certain passer-by, Simon of Cyrene who was coming in from the country, the father of Alexander and Rufus, to take up and carry his *cross*.
22 And they brought him to the "Golgotha" place (which translated is "Place of a Skull").
23 And they gave him wine spiced with myrrh, which he did not take.
24 And they *crucified* him and divided up his garments among themselves, casting lots over them to see who would take what.
25 Now it was the third hour when they *crucified* him.
26 And the inscription of the charge against him read, "The King of the Jews."
27 And with him they *crucified* two robbers, one on the right side and one on his left.

What is striking is that the word "cross" or "crucified" occurs in every other statement (the exception: 15:23), hammering at one's senses like a drum roll or a death knell.

. . . "And . . . the charge against him read, 'The King of the Jews.' "

15:29–32

The still silent Jesus is mocked again, as he had been by the soldiers in 15:16–20; it can be no coincidence that the only three instances of the verb translated as "ridiculed" or "jeering" occur in the passion/resurrection prediction in 10:34, the scene with the soldiers in 15:20, and here in 15:31. This scene is accordingly the counterpart to that earlier one in the concentric structure of this narrative of Jesus' death, and both are the realization of 10:34.

First to mock Jesus are "those who walked by" (15:29) who repeat the charge of the "false witnesses" before the council in 14:57 and taunt Jesus to "save yourself by coming down from the cross!" (15:30). Next come the "chief priests," who have been Jesus' principal adversaries since Judas' offer to betray Jesus in 14:10, with the scribes. They repeat the taunting: "Come down from the cross now" (15:32). But Mark has given their words a particular sting; having handed Jesus over to Pilate as "the King of the Jews," they now call him "the Christ, the King of Israel," but only in mockery. What they say they want is "that we might 'see' and 'believe' " (15:32), but their actions have betrayed their true feelings about Jesus and there is no real acknowledgment of Jesus as their "King" nor expectation that they will "see" in him anything in which to "believe." With these two groups Mark has wonderfully associated the two "robbers" crucified with Jesus; they also reviled Jesus (15:32). The effect of these few verses is thus to align the passers-by and the chief priests and the scribes with the two robbers! Truly it is a cadre of "ungodly men" (Wis 1:16) arrayed against Jesus, and the words of Wisdom 2 are once again appropriately realized:

> Let us see if his words are true,
>> and let us test what will happen at the end of his life;
> for if the righteous man is God's son, he will help him,
>> and will deliver him from the hand of his adversaries   (Wis 2:17–18).

15:33–38

When Mark turns from the image of all Jesus' adversaries mocking him to his account of Jesus' death, he says simply that "a darkness came over the whole earth" (15:33). It is natural to think of that darkness as the gathering of a storm about to unleash its power, either as the power of the God of Israel against Israel, which would tear the temple curtain in two when Jesus died, or as the power of the forces of evil gaining in strength as Jesus' strength ebbed.

The evocative power of the image of "darkness" is particularly strong because Mark has alluded to wisdom materials elsewhere in his gospel and certainly did so at 15:10. "Darkness" is a not uncommon image for evil in wisdom literature. In the book of Wisdom, for example, the plague of darkness Moses wrought over the land of Egypt at Yahweh's command (Ex 10:21–13) is made into an image of Yahweh's imprisonment in Wisdom 17:21:

> . . . over those men alone heavy night was spread,
>> an image of the *darkness* that was destined to receive them

and again in Wis 18:4:

> for their enemies [of Israel] deserved to be deprived of light and
>> imprisoned in *darkness*,
>> those who had kept thy sons imprisoned,
>> through whom the imperishable light of the law was to be given to
>> the world.

Yet a different use of "darkness" is found in Proverbs, where "wisdom" is spoken of as

> delivering you from the way of evil,
>> from men of perverted speech,
> who forsake the paths of uprightness
>> to walk in the ways of *darkness,*
> who rejoice in doing *evil*
>> and delight in the perverseness of evil;
> men whose paths are crooked,
>> and who are devious in their ways   (Prov 2:12–15).

Whether Mark 15:33 expresses the power of God or the essence of evil, therefore, is not clear. Perhaps the latter is to be preferred because of the preceding scene where Jesus has no power before the mocking voices of all those around him.

What also supports this is what happens next. Jesus cries out "with a loud voice" (15:34), his first words since this account of his death began in 15:2. He recites the opening words of Psalm 22: "My God, my God, why have you forsaken me?" That psalm is the cry, not of a despairing man, but of one desperate under the onslaught of affliction. Some of the verses have always seemed particularly to have come to expression in Mark's account of Jesus' death:

> All who see me mock at me,
>> they make mouths at me, they wag their heads;
> "He committed his cause to the Lord; let him deliver him,
>> let him rescue him, for he delights in him!"   (Ps 22:7–8).

> Yea, dogs are round about me;
>> a company of evil doers encircle me;
>> they have pierced my hands and feet . . .
> they divide my garments among them,
>> and for my raiment they cast lots.   (Ps 22:16–18).

But the psalm is finally an expression of complete confidence in God:

> For he has not despised or abhorred the affliction of the afflicted;
>> and he has not hid his face from him,

> but has heard, *when he cried* to him. . . .
> The afflicted shall eat and be satisfied;
>   those who seek him shall praise the Lord   (Ps 22:24–26).

The image of "darkness," therefore, is probably best understood as suggesting that the hostility and mockery of Jesus' enemies from the third hour (15:25) to the sixth hour (15:33) simply intensified until Jesus broke his silence at the ninth hour and began to cry out to the Lord in the words of Psalm 22.

Twice Mark observes that Jesus cried out "with a loud voice" (15:34, 37). If Jesus' effort to recite Psalm 22 is our guide here, this is not to be understood as a cry of pain or of desperation but as the bold and confident and forthright voice of one who has confidence in God. In Jesus are the words of Wisdom 5:1 personified:

> Then the righteous man will stand with great confidence
>   in the presence of those who have afflicted him,
>   and those who make light of his labors.

That material in Wisdom 5 goes on to speak of the righteous man being numbered among the sons of God, of his lot being among the saints (Wis 5:5), of the righteous who live for ever and whose reward is with the Lord (Wis 5:15).

When Jesus "gave up his spirit" (15:37) the immediate consequence is that "the curtain of the temple was torn in two, from top to bottom" (15:38). Jesus had been acknowledged by God as his beloved Son because Jesus had known what the Father required of men and women; he had known that the "secret" of being righteous before God was to love one's neighbor as oneself and to put oneself at the service of all. No more radical example of such a readiness to give up one's own self can be found than in giving up one's very life. Jesus has become *the* example and *the* revelation of what the Father wants of men and women. No longer, therefore, is "love of God" to be through sacrifice and burnt offering in the temple (cf. 12:29–34, especially verse 33); from now on it is to be through the sacrifice of oneself on behalf of one's "neighbor." The institution of the temple is now an empty shell, and the tearing of its curtain symbolically asserts that the barrier to true worship of God has been removed.

15:39

We have suggested that a concentric structure organizes these various parts of the narrative of Jesus' death. One scene remains to complete that pattern. If this narrative had opened in 15:2 with Pilate's question "Are you the King of the Jews?" and that title had appeared in every episode except the one reporting Jesus' death, the question had never really been answered. Now in this closing scene another non-Jew responds to Pilate's question: "Truly this man was a Son of God!" If the formal title "King of the Jews" is to be used of Jesus, it must conform to the reality of what Jesus showed himself to be on the cross: truly the "Son of God," holy and righteous, giving of himself in obedience to the Father's will, even to death.

Final Comment

In the central section of Mark's gospel (8:27–10:45), Jesus had spoken of God's will for him. The three passion/resurrection predictions had disclosed to uncomprehending disciples the very mystery of the kingdom of God, that to save one's life one must lose it. Even the Son of Man had come to put his life at the service of others.

Those predictions of Jesus' passion provided the outline for the narrative of 14:10–15:39. There Jesus is the one (and the *only* one) to perceive the Father's will for him, and he accepts it. Rejected by even his own and mocked by all, he silently accepts the afflictions heaped upon him. Even at the end of his life he is the righteous one who has poured out his own life in an act of obedience and giving which demonstrates the *new* way men and women are to live before their God. In that act of giving of himself, Jesus showed himself to be truly "righteous," truly the "Son of God." At the same time the old order of sacrifice and burnt offerings became no longer of value because "love of God" was now to be shown through "love of neighbor." The wisdom of God had replaced forever the wisdom of men.

There is one element of the passion/resurrection predictions which remains, however. In each of them Jesus had asserted that the Son of Man "will rise." Mark's story of Jesus is not yet complete.

Observations About the Gospel's Concentric Structure

In the overall concentric plan of his gospel, Mark's last major section in 14:10–15:39 corresponds to the materials found in his first major section in 1:21–3:6. Clearly the narrative of Jesus' passion elaborates the hint in 3:6 that the Pharisees and Herodians were collaborating on how to "destroy" him. Yet there are other elements on which these two sections may be compared.

1. The first major section opens with a recognition of Jesus as the "Holy One of God" by the demon in 1:24, a motif which is continued in 1:34. The passion narrative ended with the proclamation of Jesus as the "Son of God" by the centurion in 15:39.

2. Another emphasis in that first major section is that people come to Jesus from all directions; the massive popular response is a prominent feature in 1:32, 37, 45; 2:2, 13. But all that is reversed in the passion narrative, where Jesus predicts that everyone will be scandalized at him (14:27) and where "everyone abandoned him and fled" (14:50). If it is practically impossible for Jesus to be alone at the beginning of the gospel (1:35–37), he is entirely alone as he proceeds to his death.

3. In that first major section, Jesus had gone out to a desolate place, away from his disciples, in order to pray (1:35), and when he returned it was with a commitment to the mission given him, to "preach" in the towns of Israel (1:38). Similarly in the passion narrative, Jesus retreats to Gethsemane in order to pray (14:32) and returns with a renewed commitment to obey the Father's will for him (14:41).

4. In Mark 3:2 "they watched closely . . . so that they could denounce him," a motif which recurs in 14:55 where the "chief priests and the whole sanhedrin were looking for evidence against Jesus in order to put him to death."

5. And finally, the passion narrative surely elaborates Jesus' earlier, enigmatic remark that "a time will come when the bridegroom will be taken away from them . . ." (2:20). Jesus, graced with the Wisdom of God, was that bridegroom whose presence and teaching in Israel was a time for rejoicing, not fasting. But in the betrayal, rejection and death of Jesus narrated in 14:10–15:39, that bridegroom was surely taken away from Israel.

1′ The Last Interlude 15:40–47

Jesus' Last Followers

Those disciples whom Jesus had called to be "with him" and who had been privileged to have Jesus teach them privately the "secret" of the kingdom of God had all fled from him when he was seized in the garden of Gethsemane. Even staunch Peter had denied him three times shortly thereafter. These twelve who were later to "see" and "understand" seem not even to have been present at the very end of Jesus' life. But some others who had "followed him and served him" (15:41), mostly women, remained. The mention of Mary Magdalene and Mary the mother of Joses at the beginning (15:40) and end (15:47) of these verses unifies them into a single scene. Named with them, therefore, is Joseph of Arimathea "who was himself eagerly awaiting the kingdom of God" (15:43). These form a small group, "awaiting the kingdom of God," who remained followers of Jesus despite the circumstances of his death.

There can be no triumph over death, no resurrection, without death having first seemed to triumph. The burial of Jesus in the tomb is not only an act of respect and love for one who has died. It is also an expression of confidence, by a follower of Jesus, that death will be overcome. All the other "interludes" have given a particular lesson for discipleship, and 15:40–47 does so as well. Like the women, we are called to look beyond the physical reality of the death of Jesus and the mockery which following his "way" may entail, and to *remain* faithful followers. And like Joseph, ours is to be a life of "awaiting the kingdom of God," that coming of the power of the resurrection of Jesus which confirms his teaching that we are called to love one another and which enables us to do so.

Observations About the Gospel's Concentric Structure

In the overall concentric plan Mark used for his gospel, this last interlude in Mark 15:40–47 corresponds to the first interlude in Mark 1:16–20 where Jesus calls his first disciples. *Both* interludes describe the call of the disciples as having taken place "in Galilee" (1:16; 15:41) and *both* emphasize that the respective disciples "followed" Jesus there (1:18, 20; 15:41). If 1:16–20 narrates the call of Jesus' "first" disciples, 15:40–47 narrates the fidelity of those few who remained loyal to him even in the hour of his death and were his "last" disciples. This group still eagerly awaits the kingdom of God announced by Jesus in 1:15 and toward which the first disciples "followed" him.

A′ The Climax of Mark's Gospel 16:1–8

Jesus Is Confirmed as Son of God by His Resurrection

Mark's story about Jesus comes to its climax with these verses. Those women who had remained followers of Jesus to the very end of his life seek to minister to him one more time; "they bought spices in order to go and anoint him" (16:1). The problem of rolling back the "very large" stone which blocked the tomb remained a question they hadn't answered.

Yet when they arrived they find the stone already rolled back and, inside the tomb, a young man "wearing a long white robe, and they were utterly *amazed*" (16:5). That reaction of being "amazed" had been one which earlier in the gospel had indicated the radical failure of those around Jesus to understand the authority and power he exercised. Now even his last faithful followers have to be reassured by this mysterious figure: "Do *not* be amazed" (16:6). The time for amazement is now passed because God has raised his beloved Son from the dead: "He has risen! He is not here! Look at the place where they put him."

Observations About the Gospel's Concentric Structure

Just as in the opening section of this gospel (1:1–15) Jesus is attested to Mark's reader, by "a voice . . . out of the heavens" (1:11), so now in this closing section which Mark offers as the climax of his gospel the three women have an angel attest to them the reality of Jesus' being risen. And just as in that opening section Jesus would go "into Galilee" proclaiming that the "kingdom of God has come near," so does the angel tell the women to "tell his disciples, even Peter, 'He is going before you to Galilee; there you *will see* him . . .'" (16:7), because the kingdom of God has come.

Yet the most striking correspondence between Mark 1:1–15 and 16:1–8 is in the narrative of the resurrection of Jesus. Mark 1:1–15 had promised to recount the beginning of the good news about Jesus. Jesus himself announces that one should "believe in the good news (1:15). But the actual content of that good news is not given until *this* passage in 16:1–8: that humankind has in Jesus an actual instance of God's granting continuance beyond death to the righteous; until then, it had been only a hope of those who stood in the Jewish wisdom tradition that "the righteous live for ever, and their reward is with the Lord" (Wis 5:15). The resurrection of Jesus, however, now showed men and women in all ages that the Wisdom tradition's confident hope in immortality for the righteous was not a vain one. God had in fact and in human experience given confirmation to the assertion that "the righteous live for ever." And this was good news indeed, to be proclaimed everywhere.

Yet one other correspondence between Mark 1:1–15 and 16:1–8 is had as a consequence of the resurrection of Jesus. The proclamation of the angel that "He has risen! He is not here!" is the *confirmation* that Jesus was indeed the "Son of God," for it was the "righteous man," "God's Son," who was "numbered among the sons of God" in the book of Wisdom (Wis 2:12, 18; 5:5) by being granted immortality. Jesus, however, was no literary figure but the one whose story Mark relates and who in conforming his will to that of the Father's disclosed to all men and women the righteousness God wants of men. God's act in raising Jesus from the dead confirmed that righteousness and confirmed as well that Jesus was, as the centurion had come to realize, "*Truly* . . . a Son of God!" Christianity's proclamation goes further and asserts that because of God's act in raising Jesus from the dead, Jesus is confirmed as *the* paradigm of righteousness for men and women: he is *the* Son of God! And in this emphasis on Jesus as "Son of God" we have yet another correspondence with Mark 1:1–15; the angel's proclamation of Jesus' resurrection (16:6) is the direct counterpart to the declaration of the voice from heaven at Jesus' baptism, "You are my beloved Son; with you I am well pleased" (1:11).

In these respects, 16:1–8 brings the concentric pattern begun in 1:1–15 to a fitting climax.

Mk 16:1–8 and the Wisdom of Solomon

Until early Christianity's experience of Jesus as raised from the dead, the illustration of the kind of righteousness which God would reward with immortality was the story in the Wisdom of Solomon of the man who "boasts that God is his father" (Wis 2:16) so that he could aptly be called "God's son" (Wis 2:18). One finds in the Wisdom of Solomon the sharpest possible contrast between the "righteous man" (2:12) who is "God's son" (2:18) and the "ungodly men" in their respective convictions about death. For the "ungodly men," a description of the finality of death and of the futility of life in Wisdom 2:2–4 is begun with an assertion that death is the absolute end in Wisdom 2:1,

> Short and sorrowful is our life,
>> and there is no remedy when a man comes to his end,
>> and no one has been known to return from Hades.

But the "righteous man," on the other hand, "calls the last end of the righteous happy" (Wis 2:16), a judgment with which the author of the Wisdom of Solomon agrees. While the "ungodly men" "lie in wait" (Wis 2:12) for the righteous man, to "test him with insult and torture" and to "condemn him to a shameful death" (Wis 2:20) out of "envy" (Wis 2:24), they are the ones finally who are "shaken with a dreadful fear," and "amazed at his unexpected salvation" (Wis 5:2). And they give voice to the condemnation of their evil ways which the immortality of the righteous man represents (Wis 5:4–6). Yet the author of the Wisdom of Solomon thinks not only of the one righteous man whose story he tells in Wisdom 2–5, but of all the righteous "numbered among the sons of God." According to the "secret purposes of God" (Wis 2:22), "the righteous live for ever and their reward is with the Lord" (Wis 5:15). The confident assertions of the immortality of the righteous, however, had to have remained just that, for human experience would have had to acknowledge the point made by the ungodly men (Wis 2:5):

> Our allotted time is the passing of a shadow,
>> and there is no return from our death,
>> because it is sealed up and no one turns back.

But now, in Jesus' resurrection, humankind has had direct experience of God's granting immortality to a man, of God's approving a man as "righteous." As we have noted, Mark's story of Jesus in many respects replicates the story of the righteous man and the hostility he experienced from the "ungodly." Yet Jesus, far more than the literary figure in Wisdom 2:12–20, is the righteous one who can be called "God's Son." The voice from the heavens declared to Jesus, and announced to the reader of Mark's gospel, that Jesus was to be God's "beloved Son" (1:11), and the voice of the angel at the tomb announced to all that God had indeed rewarded with immortality the righteousness which Jesus sought to teach Israel was the will of God for humankind: "He is risen! He is not here! Look at the place where they put him!"

16:8—Mark's Final Comment

It has often been observed, however, that the actual last verse of the gospel, 16:8, seems an odd note on which to bring this elaborately conceived literary work to its conclusion. The women "went out and fled from the tomb; for a trembling and a bewilderment possessed them, and they said nothing to anyone, for they were afraid." Several considerations diminish the oddity of that ending. First of all, that the women "said nothing to anyone, for they were afraid" prevents the emptiness of the tomb in Jerusalem from being the basis for proclaiming the resurrection; faith rests not upon there being no body in the tomb but upon "seeing" Jesus risen. Second, it affirms that until one has personally "seen" the risen Jesus, one can only react humanly and naturally and with "fear." Jesus had often asked his disciples not to be afraid, but they could not *but* be afraid, since they had not yet experienced the coming of the kingdom of God in power that was his resurrection. No amount of proclaiming that Jesus is "risen," (even by an angel!) will bring the faith response that "seeing" the risen Jesus will occasion. Third, this ending to Mark's gospel respects the tradition that it was to Peter that the risen Jesus first appeared; the angel's assurance that "he is going before you to Galilee; there you will see him" looks forward to the coming of Peter and the other disciples to "see" and understand what "the rising from the dead" meant, as he had assured them they would in Mark 9:9f.

The scene with which Mark ends his gospel is not a story of a resurrection appearance, therefore, but a proclamation of the fact of Jesus' resurrection. For Mark, that is enough. There is no incongruity to the gospel's ending. Mark had only promised to tell his reader the *beginning* of the *good news*. That good news is now proclaimed to all by the angel: "The crucified Jesus of Nazareth . . . has risen! He is not here!" (16:6). Mark has done what he had said he would do. It is now for his reader to decide whether to remain "amazed" and "afraid," or to go where he is and "see" him.

Conclusion: From Story to Theology

We have read with close attention the story which Mark has told about Jesus. A large, concentric structure seemed to have organized the materials which Mark presented, and that structure serves graphically to underscore the reversal of human expectations by what is "of God"; for "many who are first . . . will be last, and the last, first" (10:31). Perhaps a good place to start this chapter's effort at a summary expression of Mark's theology, therefore, would be back at its opening verse. There clearly and directly Mark has addressed you, his reader. He has indicated succinctly what his book will be about: "the *beginning* of the *good news* [gospel] about Jesus Christ, the *Son of God*." Those three terms are tersely interwoven; each needs an elaboration of its development in Mark's gospel. Let us start with the "good news!"

So accustomed are we to the word "gospel" as a reference to the writings of Matthew, Mark, Luke and John that we may forget that behind that word is a word in Greek which needs an exclamation point, the "good news!" When early Christianity preached the "gospel," it proclaimed the "good news!" that the followers of Jesus could get excited about, shout and sing about, even die for. Just what does Mark tell us is the "good news"?

The angel at the empty tomb gives us part of that "good news!": "The crucified Jesus of Nazareth . . . has risen . . . you will see him!" (16:7). But that is not all; Jesus' resurrection is but "the beginning." For throughout the gospel Jesus has proclaimed the "kingdom of God" to be a reality accessible to those who know its "secret." Jesus' resurrection was the first realization of that long-held conviction that God would approve the righteous man in an ultimate way. Perhaps these ideas could be brought together in this expression of Mark's "good news!": In the kingdom of God the righteous "son of God" (first Jesus, and then those who would follow him) will be raised from the dead.

The "good news," then is the affirmation of resurrection as a reality accessible to those who are righteous before God. What the book of Wisdom affirmed for the righteous man, who called God his Father, and for all the "holy ones" is confirmed in Jesus! It is no longer open to question by Sadducees or anyone else.

The resurrection is a prominent theme in Mark, although it may not always be explicitly apparent. Let us begin our examination of this theme by noting that the earlier Mark's gospel is dated and the more Jewish the context which is assumed for its composition, the more the evidence which can be brought to bear to support this theme. If the gospel were composed by a Greek-speaking, Jewish follower of Jesus, residing in an area of the diaspora beyond Israel and addressing an audience of Hellenistic Jews, we would have no different a situation from that reflected in the speeches in Acts 2 and 3, except that it would be located in the Greek-speaking world; indeed, the speech Peter gives on the occasion of Pentecost in Acts 2 is addressed to "men from every nation under heaven" (Acts 2:5; cf. 2:8–11). The Jewish scriptures which would be authoritative for them would include two pieces of wisdom literature, the Wisdom of Solomon and the book of Sirach. Against the background particularly of Wisdom 2:12–5:8, Mark's reference to Jesus as the "Son of God" would have been particularly suggestive; it would have been an identification of Jesus with the righteous man (Wis 2:12) who is God's son (Wis 2:18), and it would have evoked the central affirmation of the book of Wisdom, i.e. that the righteous man will have a continuance after death, that "the righteous man who has died will condemn the ungodly who are living" (Wis 4:16). In order to see these parallels more clearly, the Appendix has placed the story told about Wisdom (cf. the Introduction, pp. 17–23) and texts from the Wisdom of Solomon and the gospel of Mark side by side.

And so resurrection is implicitly part of the "good news" right from Mark's first use of the title "Son of God" for Jesus in 1:1. It would have been reinforced by the voice from heaven which addressed Jesus, "You are my beloved Son; with you I am well pleased," because Jesus was the realization of Wisdom 4:10: "There was one who pleased God and was loved by him" (see also Wis 4:14).

Resurrection is explicitly in focus in the three predictions which stand out like diamonds on black velvet in Mark's central section, 8:27–10:45; each of them ends with the assurance that the Son of Man "will rise" as its climax. Moreover, if our interpretation of 9:1 is correct, the reference to the coming of the kingdom of God "in power" also refers to the resurrection; certainly what follows in 9:2–8 repeats the identification of Jesus as God's "beloved Son," as implicit an affirmation of the possibility of resurrection as had been the voice from heaven at the baptism. Resurrection is also explicitly affirmed in what immediately follows in 9:9–10, when Jesus cautions the three disciples not to tell anyone what they had seen "until the Son of Man had risen from the dead," and they question what "rising from the dead" meant.

Resurrection is also explicitly in focus when Jesus is confronted by the Sadducees in 12:18–27. Mark immediately identifies them as "the ones who say there isn't a resurrection" (12:18) and ends the confrontation with Jesus' affirmation that God "is not God of the dead, but of the living! You are very wrong."

When Jesus is asked by the high priest if he is "the Son of the Blessed One" (14:61), Jesus acknowledges that he is and expresses the full conviction of the righteous man that God will vindicate him (14:62), an implicit reference to resurrection. When Jesus is on the cross, his beginning to recite Psalm 22 (15:34) with its confident expectation that God will come to the aid of the afflicted also continues this theme, particularly when only five verses later the centurion exclaims, "Truly this man was a Son of God!" (15:39).

Finally, that theme is made explicit in the words of the angel at the empty tomb: "Jesus of Nazareth . . . has risen!" (16:6). No more explicit statement can be made than that one. Coming at the end of Mark's gospel, it returns to what the "Son of God" reference had suggested at its beginning and it confirms what the reader of Mark's gospel had expected from the various references the evangelist had made.

The reality of Jesus' resurrection, therefore, is intimately a part of the good news Mark tells his reader about. And yet that one man, however righteous, should have been raised from the dead is not enough to be called good news unless it has opened up a new possibility for others as well. This is where it is appropriate, therefore, to summarize what Mark calls the *"kingdom of God."*

The phrase "kingdom of God" first appears in Mark 1:15. Jesus had been acknowledged by the voice from heaven as God's beloved Son in 1:11. Then in 1:12–13 Mark tells us of Jesus' being "tested by Satan" and ministered to by angels, a scene reminiscent of Wisdom 3:5, "God tested them [the righteous] and found them worthy of himself," and Wisdom 4:14, "His soul was pleasing to the Lord, therefore he took him quickly from the midst of wickedness." If the temptation of Jesus narrative is also an allusion to the book of Wisdom and an anticipation of the description of Jesus' passion, then a resurrection motif is also implicitly present in the verses which separate 1:11 from Jesus' entrance into Galilee and his first proclamation of the kingdom of God. Yet, even without that interpretation of the temptation account, Jesus' proclamation of the kingdom of God in 1:14–15 is closely associated with Jesus' being the beloved Son and the motif of resurrection.

Just what is the "kingdom of God"? The phrase itself eliminates the possibility that this is a reality man can establish from this world on his own initiative; this is "of God." Again what is characteristic of that kingdom may be understood by reference to the book of Wisdom, where all dominion and sovereignty come from God (Wis 6:3). Wisdom 6:4 describes the error of those who will be judged terribly and swiftly because

> you did not rule rightly,
> nor keep the law,
> nor walk according to the purpose of God   (Wis 6:4).

The kingdom of God then is characterized by "walking according to the purpose of God." The harshness of Jesus' rebuke of Peter in 8:33 is explained in terms of precisely that opposition: "You are not committed to the things of God, but to the things of men!" But if Jesus walks "on the side of God," it is not easy for others to do so. When Jesus teaches "how difficult it is for those who have possessions to enter into the kingdom of God" (10:23) and the disciples wonder "Then who *can* be saved?" (10:26), Jesus' response is pointed: "With men it is impossible, but not with God, for everything is possible with God" (10:27). Since the things which are "of men" prevail and walking according to the purpose of God must be enabled by the power of God, the kingdom of God must be to some extent future. But Jesus proclaims it to have "come near" in 1:15!

Just before Jesus' parable of the sower in Mark 4:1–9, Jesus exclaims, "Whoever does the will of God, *that person* is my brother and sister and mother" (3:35). The parables of Mark 4 then describe the kingdom of God as the corporate reality of the ones "who hear 'the word' and embrace it and 'bear fruit' " (4:20). The disciples of Jesus are to be a part of that corporate reality, for to them "is given the secret of the kingdom of God" (4:11). But that corporate reality will grow and increase in size as more and more come to it; it is like the grain of mustard seed which "becomes the largest of all the herbs . . . so that the birds of the air can settle in its shade" (4:31–32).

Just what is the "secret" of the kingdom of God? How can people "hear the word and embrace it"? How can one know what the "will of God" requires so that he can do it? That is the question which Mark answers in his story of Jesus' suffering and death. Placed squarely in the middle of the concentric organization of the gospel is the insistence of Jesus that to save one's life, one must lose it (8:35). His own acceptance of the Father's will (the effect of the "must" in 8:31) that he give up his life is made the model and paradigm and fundamental teaching of the "secret" of entering into the kingdom of God. No simpler statement of the reversal of human expectations can be found than the statement with which that section of the gospel ended: "For the Son of Man did not come to be served, but to serve and to give his life as a ransom for many" (10:45). In the corporate reality that is the kingdom of God, all men and women must put themselves at the service of each other; in this will they be "of God" and unique like "salt," if they live "at peace with one another" (9:50).

There is another place where Jesus gives expression to this same idea. When asked by one of the scribes, "Which is the most important commandment of all?" (12:28), Jesus' response is that one must "love the Lord your God" and "love your neighbor like yourself" (12:29–30). He then continues: "There is no other commandment than these." It seems at first as though Jesus has cited two commandments, but what follows is instructive; the scribe couples the two commandments into one single effort: "to love him with all the heart . . . *and* to love one's neighbor like oneself, *is* (singular!) far better than all the whole burnt offerings . . ." (12:33). That answer Jesus approves: "You are not far from the kingdom of God" (12:34). For if entering the kingdom of God is dependent upon doing the will of God, and the will of God is that we love our neighbor, then the commitment to that ethic of service and love of neighbor is at the same time love of God. The two are inseparably linked. It is through the giving up of self to further the good of others that we enter into the kingdom of God. That is the reversal of what we naturally think; for it is all too human to assert ourselves over against others. Yet this is precisely why Jesus can speak of it as the "secret" of the kingdom of God.

What is of God cannot be deduced by men nor practiced by men on their own initiative. It must be revealed and enabled by God. In Mark both the revelation and the enabling occur through Jesus. And it is that which is the good news. That we now know what God requires of men for them to be righteous before him. And that in Jesus' resurrection all have confirmation of that revelation and the power to be able to live committed to the ethic of love and service for others.

Who, then, is this Jesus? To know that he is the "Son of God" is to know, in the context again of the book of Wisdom, that "he professes to have knowledge of God" (Wis 2:13). That is amply demonstrated in Mark. In the first scene of Jesus' public ministry, for example, it is asserted that "they were amazed at his teaching, for he was teaching them like one who had authority and not the way the scribes taught" (1:21). That Jesus was "teaching" recurs like a refrain time and again in the gospel, and in episode after episode he is shown authoritatively interpreting "the commandment of God" and disentangling it from "the tradition of men" (7:8). After a challenge to his authority (11:27–33), when challenged about what is "lawful," he is addressed by some Pharisees and Herodians who admit this: "Teacher, we know that you are honest . . . and do not consider the outward appearance of persons, but in truth teach the way of God" (12:13). And it is in that context that Jesus says, "The things which belong to Caesar, give to Caesar; but the things which belong to God, give to God" (12:17).

But if Jesus is the "Son of God," the "righteous man" who "has knowledge of God," then he is also one who stands in a special relation to God's "Wisdom." In the book of Wisdom, Wisdom is spoken of as though it were an independent personage. It is she who "passes into holy souls and makes them friends of God" (Wis 7:27); indeed, there is a special and intimate bond between Wisdom and those who have found her (cf. e.g. Wis 6:12–16 and 8:16–18). And in Mark 6:30–8:21 the portrayal of Jesus is even colored by the portrayal of Wisdom in Proverbs 8:1–9:6, Wisdom 8, and Sirach 1 and 24, as we have seen.

That association of Jesus, the "Son of God," with the portrayal of Wisdom suggests that to speak of Jesus simply as the "righteous Son of God" was not enough of an identification. Questions about the identification of Jesus abound in the gospel and are resolved one after another. The scribes suggest that he is possessed by Beelzebul (3:22), a charge which Jesus reasons out of existence and condemns as an unforgivable blasphemy (3:23–30). After the stilling of the storm episode the disciples in the boat with Jesus ask pointedly, "Who then *is* this, that even wind and sea obey him?" (4:41). In 8:27 Jesus asks "Who do people say that I am?" and he is given three responses: John the Baptist, Elijah, one of the prophets. Peter adds a fourth: "You are the Christ." In the narrative which follows,

Jesus deflects that fourth identification (8:30) and then is shown dramatically to be neither Elijah nor Moses (the greatest of the prophets) in 9:2–8, nor the Baptist in 9:13. At the beginning of his controversies with the religious leaders in Jerusalem, the chief priests and scribes and elders ask by what authority he does his mighty works. Jesus himself raises the question of who "the Christ" is and suggests that he must be something more than simply the "son of David" (12:35–37). He is asked by the high priest "Are you the Christ, the Son of the Blessed One?" (14:61) and responds "I am" (14:62). But when Pilate later asks him "Are you the King of the Jews?" (15:2), Jesus really refuses to accept that isolated identification. As we saw, it is the centurion at the foot of the cross who provides the real answer to Pilate's question: this is not simply the "king of the Jews," but "truly this man was a Son of God!" (15:39).

Questions about *who* Jesus is abound because as the righteous Son of God Jesus knows what is pleasing to God, has been taught by Wisdom, and participates in the mysterious authority which Wisdom gives. Just as Wisdom knows "what is secret and what is manifest" (Wis 7:21), so does Jesus know the "secret" of the kingdom of God, that "wisdom" which is God's will for men and women. Just as Wisdom reaches out to teach to others what is pleasing to God (Wis 6:12–13), so does Jesus call to himself those whom he desired (3:13) to teach them privately time and again what they must do to enter into the kingdom of God. To think of Jesus as simply a righteous man is not enough. He is the righteous one, "the Holy One of God" (1:24), the embodiment of the Wisdom of God who can teach his disciples what is pleasing to God. From the account of Jesus' baptism on, the reader of Mark's gospel observes that Jesus' ministry to Israel is one graced by the presence of the Spirit, or Wisdom, of God.

If this summary has elaborated the meaning of the good news and of Jesus, the "Son of God," in Mark 1:1, there remains one other part of that verse to comment upon. What does Mark mean by *the beginning . . .*"?

In the Markan perspective the story he tells comes to its fruition in the resurrection of Jesus. As 9:9 indicates, the resurrection is a turning point. That event alters the course of the situation of men irrevocably, for it confirms the truth of what Jesus taught as the righteousness expected by God. It is just not possible for the disciples accompanying Jesus to escape from the normal and human understanding of things, as we have seen several times, but particularly in 8:27–10:45. Indeed, one of the twelve betrays Jesus and the rest desert him; even Peter will not confess that he knows him, and none of them seem to have been present at the crucifixion.

The resurrection, however, reverses not just human expectations. It is the "coming" of the kingdom of God "in power," enabling the disciples to "see" Jesus and to embrace what he taught about the kingdom of God; it is a reversal of the human weakness of the disciples as well, therefore.

The story of Jesus is thus but "the beginning" of the story of the kingdom of God because it precedes Jesus' resurrection and the arrival of the kingdom in power. When Jesus came into Galilee, he preached that the kingdom of God was "at hand." After the resurrection, the angel instructs the women to tell the disciples that Jesus "is going before you to Galilee; there you will see him" (16:7). Finally their blindness will be turned into sight and their failure to understand into understanding.

And so, what Mark wanted his reader to know he succinctly drew together in the phrasings of his first verse. But why did this evangelist labor so over his story about Jesus? Because it is not just a story about Jesus "the Son of God" or about the "beginning" of the "good news" and the "kingdom of God." It is also an address, an appeal to his reader, in whatever age. Mark wanted his reader to see and perceive, hear and understand (cf. 4:10–12), to be "salt," to take up the cross of service and love of others, to follow on the way like once-blind Bartimaeus, to look for the kingdom of God like the women and Joseph of Arimathea, to cry out with the centurion an acknowledgment of Jesus as the Son of God, to "see" the risen Jesus and enter into the power of the kingdom of God. Jesus' words at the end of the parable of the sower were a challenge to each of us as well: "Whoever has ears to hear, let him hear!" (4:9).

We started by observing that the gospel of Mark was "deceptive" because its simplicity of expression masked an interpretation of Jesus' importance for men, a "theology," which was hardly a "simple" one. It seems an appropriate ending to these comments to repeat that appraisal of the gospel as "deceptive." For it is not just a story; it is as well an appeal and a challenge to "repent! And believe in the good News" (1:15). One cannot read the gospel of Mark without being challenged to choose between what is "of men" and what is "of God." And in that, finally, rests its deceptive power.

Appendix: "Wisdom" and the Wisdom of Solomon and Parallels in the Gospel of Mark

The Wisdom Myth	Wisdom of Solomon	Mark	Mark
Wisdom was present at the creation of the world	9:9 With thee is wisdom, who knows thy works and was present when thou didst make the world		
and indeed was the agent through whom God created it.	7:22 ... Wisdom, the fashioner of all things ...		
Her place is beside God	8:3–4 She glorifies her noble birth by living with God, and the Lord of all loves her. For she is an initiate in the knowledge of God, and an associate in his works.		
	9:9–10 With thee is Wisdom. . . . Send her forth from the holy heavens and from the throne of thy glory send her ...	1:10 And ... he saw the heavens being split apart,	
and she is a "holy" spirit	7:22–24 For in her there is a spirit that is intelligent, holy, unique, manifold, subtle, mobile,		

The Wisdom Myth	Wisdom of Solomon	Mark	Mark
	clear, unpolluted, distinct, invulnerable, loving the good, keen, irresistible, beneficent humane, steadfast, sure, free from anxiety, all powerful, and penetrating through all spirits that are intelligent and pure and most subtle. For wisdom is more mobile than any motion; because of her pureness she pervades and penetrates all things.		
	Cf. 9:17 below— Who has learned thy counsel, unless thou hast given Wisdom and sent thy holy Spirit from on high?	and the Spirit coming down upon him like a dove, and a voice came out of the heavens,	
and her transcendence of and authority over the created world is complete.	7:22–8:1. Cf. esp. 7:25–27b, For she is a breath of the power of God, and a pure emanation of the glory of the Almighty; therefore nothing defiled gains entrance into her. For she is a reflection of eternal light, a spotless mirror of the		

The Wisdom Myth	Wisdom of Solomon	Mark	Mark
	working of God, and an image of his goodness. Though she is but one, she can do all things, and while remaining in herself, she renews all things . . .		
	8:1 She reaches mightily from one end of the earth to the other and she orders all things well.		
Although to men the will of God seems hidden and concealed,	2:22 (the ungodly) did not know the secret purposes of God . . .		
	9:13–17 . . . what man can learn the counsel of God? Or who can discern what the Lord wills? For the reasoning of mortals is worthless, and our designs are likely to fail, for a perishable body weights down the soul, and this earthy tent burdens the thoughtful mind. We can hardly guess at what is on earth . . . but who has traced out what is the		

The Wisdom Myth	Wisdom of Solomon	Mark	Mark
	heavens? Who has learned thy counsel?		
Wisdom knows what God requires of men and women	7:21–22 I learned both what is secret and what is manifest, for Wisdom, the fashioner of all things, taught me.		
	9:9–11 With thee is Wisdom, who knows thy works . . . and who understands what is pleasing in thy sight and what is right according to thy commandments . . . she knows and understands all things. (Cf. also 9:18 below.)		
God must accordingly send Wisdom to humankind in order to teach them what is pleasing to God, to save them.	9:10–12 Send her forth from the holy heavens . . . that I may learn what is pleasing to thee. For she knows and understands all things, and she will guide me wisely in my actions and guard me with her glory. Then my works will be acceptable . . .		
	9:17–18 Who has learned thy		

The Wisdom Myth	Wisdom of Solomon	Mark	Mark
	counsel, unless thou hast given wisdom and sent thy holy Spirit from on high? And thus the paths of those on earth were set right, and men were taught what pleases thee, and were saved by wisdom.		
	8:21 I perceived that I would not possess Wisdom unless God gave her to me . . .		
Wisdom, therefore, goes about looking for worthy persons and in every age she enters into holy individuals, making them friends of God,	6:16 She (Wisdom) goes about seeking those worthy of her, and she graciously appears to them in their paths, and meets them in every thought.	"You are my beloved Son; with you I am well pleased."	
	7:27 in every generation she passes into holy souls and makes them friends of God and prophets.		
	[Cf. 1:4, where Wisdom "will *not* enter a deceitful soul, nor dwell in a body enslaved in sin."]		
and granting	8:16–18 When I		

The Wisdom Myth	Wisdom of Solomon	Mark	Mark
her disciples a life of blessings and immortality and understanding,	enter my house, I [Solomon] shall find rest with her [Wisdom], for companionship with her has no bitterness and life with her has no pain, but gladness and joy. When I considered these things inwardly, and thought upon them in my mind, that in kinship with Wisdom there is immortality, and in friendship with her, pure delight, and in the labors of her hands, unfailing wealth, and in the experience of her company, understanding, and renown in sharing her words, I went about seeking how to get her for myself.		
but she will not forgive a blasphemer.	1:6 For Wisdom . . . will not free a blasphemer from the guilt of his words.		
Thus the *righteous man* opposes the actions of the	2:12–14, 16. Let us lie in wait for the righteous man, because he is	8:15 And he instructed them, "Look! Beware of the leaven of the	11:27–28 And while he was walking about in the temple, there came

The Wisdom Myth	Wisdom of Solomon	Mark	Mark
ungodly	inconvenient to us and opposes our actions.	Pharisees and the leaven of Herod." 12:38–40 And in his teaching he said: "Watch out for the scribes who like to walk around in long robes ... These men who devour the estates of widows, and pray a long time for show, will receive a more severe condemnation!"	to him chief priests and scribes and elders, and they said to him, "With what authority do you do these things? Or who has given to you such authority that you should do these things?" 12:1–12, esp. 12:12. And they sought to seize him, even though they feared the crowd, for they knew that he told this parable against them ...
and reproaches them for sins against the law	He reproaches us for sins against the law, and accuses us of sins against our training.	Cf 10:2–9, esp. v. 5, and 11:17. Also: 7:6–13 But he said to them [Pharisees and scribes], "Well did Isaiah prophesy about you hypocrites ... when, neglecting the commandment of God, you observe the commandment of men." And he said to them, "How well you get around the commandment of God ... invalidating the word of God with your teaching which you hand on;	12:14–17, 18–27 [Pharisees and Herodians] came and said to him, "... is it permissible to give a poll-tax to Caesar or not?" ... But Jesus, knowing their hypocrisy, said to them ... "The things which belong to Caesar, give to Caesar; but the things which belong to God, give to God!" And there came to him Sadducees ... Jesus said to them, "Isn't it

The Wisdom Myth	Wisdom of Solomon	Mark	Mark
		and many such similar things do you do."	because you know neither the scriptures nor the power of God that you are wrong? ... He is not God of the dead, but of the living! You are *very* wrong."
and professes to have knowledge of God	He professes to have knowledge of God,	7:14–23 And again calling the crowd to him, he said to them, "Everyone listen to me and understand! There is nothing which goes into a man from outside him which can make him unclean; but the things which come out of a man are the things which make him unclean." 4:11 And he said to them: "To *you* is given the secret of the kingdom of God . . ." 8:31 "and he began to teach them. "The son of Man must suffer many things . . ." 8:34–38 And calling the crowd to himself, with his disciples, he said to them, ". . .	Cf. 12:24, 27 above. 12:28–34 And one of the scribes ... asked ... "Which is the most important commandment of all?" Jesus answered ... There is no commandment greater than these." And the scribe said, "Quite right, Teacher ..." And Jesus, seeing that he had spoken with understanding, said to him, "You are not far from the Kingdom of God." 10:17–27 A man ran up to him ... and asked him, "Good Teacher, what shall I do so that I may inherit eternal life?" ... And Jesus ... said to him, "There is

The Wisdom Myth	Wisdom of Solomon	Mark	Mark
		whoever destroys his life because of me and because of the good news will save it .... For whoever is ashamed of me and of my words ... the son of Man will also be ashamed of him when he comes in the glory of his Father ..."	one thing you don't have: Go, sell whatever you have and give to the poor, and you will have a treasure in heaven ..." And looking around, Jesus said to his disciples, "How difficult it is for those who have possessions to enter into the kingdom of God! ... With men it is impossible, but not with God, for everything is possible with God."
and calls him—self a "child of the Lord"	and calls himself a child of the Lord.	11:2–3, 9 [Jesus] said to them, "Go ... you will find a colt ... untie it .... And if anyone should say to you, 'Why ... ?' say, 'The Lord has need of it ...'" And those who went ahead and those who followed shouted, "Hosanna! Blessed is he who comes in the name of the Lord ..." Cf. also 12:35–37.	13:32 "However, concerning that day or the hour, no one knows, not the angels in heaven, nor the Son, but only the Father. 14:61–62. Again the high priest questioned him and said to him, "Are you the Christ, the Son of the Blessed One?" But Jesus said, "I am ..."
and avoids the ways of the ungodly as	We are considered by him as something base,	Cf. 7:1–23, esp. 7:6, and 12:13–17, esp. 12:15.	8:15 And he instructed them, "Look! Beware of

The Wisdom Myth	Wisdom of Solomon	Mark	Mark
unclean.	and he avoids our ways as unclean;		the leaven of the Pharisees and the leaven of Herod."
He can call the last end of the righteous happy	he calls the last end of the righteous happy,	8:34 "If anyone wants to follow after me [understood as resurrection], let him deny himself . . . and follow me." Cf. 8:35 above. Cf. also 12:24–27 above.	13:20, 27 "For the sake of *the elect* whom he chose, he has shortened the days. . . . And then he will send out the angels and he will gather together [his] *elect* from the four quadrants, from the end of the earth to the end of the sky."
and boast that God is his Father.	and boasts that God is his Father.	14:36 And he said, "Abba, Father, everything is possible to you . . ." Cf. 14:61–62 above.	
So the ungodly lie in wait for him,	Wis 2:12 Let us lie in wait for the righteous man . . .	3:2, 6 And they watched him closely whether he would heal him on the sabbath, so that they could denounce him . . . And the Pharisees went away and immediately formed a plan with the Herodians against him in order that they might destroy him.	12:13 And they sent to him some of the Pharisees and some of the Herodians to find a mistake in what he was teaching.
		11:18 And the high priests and the scribes . . . were seeking how to destroy him, for the	14:1 . . . and the chief priests and scribes were looking for a way to arrest and kill

The Wisdom Myth	Wisdom of Solomon	Mark	Mark
		crowd was overwhelmed at his teaching.	him in some cunning way . . . 14:55 But the chief priests and the whole sanhedrin were looking for evidence against Jesus in order to put him to death . . .
to test him with insult and torture,	Wis 2:19–20 Let us test him with insult and torture,	Cf. episodes in 11:27–33, 12:1–12, 12:13–17, and 12:18–27. Note esp. 12:15, "Why put me to the test?"	14:65 And some began to spit upon him and to blindfold his face and to strike him and say to him, "Prophesy!" and the servants treated him to slaps. 15:17–20 And they dressed him in purple; and they twisted together a crown of thorns and put it on him and began to salute him, "Hail, King of the Jews." And they struck his head with a reed and spit on him, and kneeling they paid homage to him. And when they had ridiculed him, they . . . led him out in order to crucify him.

The Wisdom Myth	Wisdom of Solomon	Mark	Mark
and to find out how gentle he is	that we may find out how gentle he is	15:4–5 Pilate again questioned him, saying, "Are you not going to answer anything? See how many things they accuse you of!" But Jesus still answered nothing, so that Pilate wondered.	
and to make trial of his forbearance.	and make a trial of his forbearance.	15:29–32 And those who walked by abused him . . . and the high priests, too, jeering among themselves and with the scribes, "Let the Christ . . . come down from the cross now, so that we might 'see' and 'believe'!" And those who were crucified with him taunted him.	
The ungodly thus condemn him to a shameful death	Let us condemn him to a shameful death,	14:63–64 The high priest . . . tore apart his tunic and said, ". . . you have heard the blasphemy. . . ." All the others then judged him to be deserving of death. 15:1 . . . the chief priests held council with the elders and scribes and the whole sanhedrin	

The Wisdom Myth	Wisdom of Solomon	Mark	Mark
		. . . and handed him over to Pilate.	
		15:15 Pilate . . . handed Jesus over to be crucified.	
	For according to what he says he will be protected.	15:29 Those who walked by abused him . . . saying, ". . . you who would pull down the temple and build it in three days, save yourself by coming down from the cross!"	
out of envy	Wis 2:24 . . . through the devil's envy death entered the world, and those who belong to his party experience it.	15:10 (For he [Pilate] knew the chief priests had handed him over because of envy.)	
for they did not know the secret purposes of God, that the righteous should have immortality.	Wis 2:22–23 . . . they did not know the secret purposes of God, nor hope for the wages of holiness, nor discern the prize for blameless souls; for God created man for incorruption, and made him in the image of his own eternity.	4:11–12 And he said to them: "To *you* is given the secret of the kingdom of God; but to those who are outside everything comes in parables, that 'Seeing, they see and do not perceive, and hearing, they hear and do not understand, lest they should turn back and it be forgiven them.' "	6:6 And he [Jesus] marveled at their lack of faith. Cf. the theme of 8:27–10:45, generally. Note esp. contrast in 8:33; cf. also 9:19: "O unbelieving generation, how long will I be with you: how long will I put up with you?"

The Wisdom Myth	Wisdom of Solomon	Mark	Mark
		10:26–27 But they were . . . saying, "Then who can be saved?" . . . Jesus said, "With men it is impossible, but not with God, for everything is possible with God."	Note the theme of God's will for Jesus implied in 8:31; then Jesus' prayer in 14:36. ("Abba, Father, everything is possible to you; take this cup away from me! But, not what I will, but what you will . . .") And note also the resolution of that scene in 14:41. ("The hour has come. Behold, the Son of Man is betrayed into the hands of sinners.")
And when, after the death of the righteous man, they are confronted with the fact of his immortality,	Wis 4:16 The righteous man who has died will condemn the ungodly who are living . . . Wis 5:1 Then the righteous man will stand with great confidence in the presence of those who have afflicted him . . .	8:39–9:1 "For whoever is ashamed of me and of my words in this adulterous and sinful generation, the Son of Man will also be ashamed of him when he comes in the glory of his Father with the holy angels." And he said to them, "Amen I say to you: There are some standing here who will not taste death until they see the kingdom of God come in power!"	
they will	Wis 5:2 When they	16:5, 8. And when	

The Wisdom Myth	Wisdom of Solomon	Mark	Mark
experience fear and amazement	see him, they will be shaken with dreadful fear, and they will be amazed at his unexpected salvation.	they went into the tomb, they saw a young man sitting on the right side, wearing a long white robe, and they were utterly amazed. . . . And they went out and fled from the tomb, for a trembling and a bewilderment possessed them, and they said nothing to anyone, for they were afraid.	
and will have to acknowledge that he is a "son of God,"	Wis 5:5 Why has he been numbered among the sons of God? And why is his lot among the saints?		15:29–39 And those who walked by abused him . . . and the high priests, too, jeering . . . and with the scribes, said . . . and those who were crucified with him taunted him . . . . But when the centurion who stood facing him saw that he had given up his spirit in this way, he said "Truly this man was a Son of God!"
because he (the righteous man) knew the "way of truth"	Wis 5:6 So it was we who strayed from the way of truth, and the light of righteousness did not shine on us . . .	Notice that Jesus (and his disciples) are "on the way" in 8:3, 8:27, 9:33, 9:34, 10:32 and 10:52. That is then further specified	8:33 But turning around . . . he rebuked Peter, saying, "Get out of my sight, Satan! Because you are not committed to

The Wisdom Myth	Wisdom of Solomon	Mark	Mark
		in 12:14: And they came and said to him, "Teacher, we know that you . . . in truth teach the way of God; . . ."	the things of God, but to the things of men" [and this in the context of being "on the way" in 8:27].
while they (the unrighteous) did not know the "way of the Lord."	Wis 5:7 We took our fill of the paths of lawlessness and destruction . . . but the way of the Lord we have not known.		
What God intends (and Wisdom discloses) is that the entire world be his "kingdom" and that all in his kingdom "walk according to the purpose of God," learning "wisdom" and being made "holy."	Wis 6:1–10 Listen therefore, 0 kings, and understand. . . . Give ear, you that rule over multitudes and boast of many nations. For your dominion was given you from the Lord . . . who will search out your works and inquire into your plans. Because as servants of his kingdom you did not rule rightly, nor keep the law, nor walk according to the purpose of God, he will come upon you terribly and swiftly. . . . For the lowliest man may be pardoned in mercy, but mighty men will be mightily tested. . . .	(Cf. context in 10:35–41:) 10:42–45, Jesus said to them, "You know 'those who seem to rule over the Gentiles lord it over them,' and 'their rulers wield authority over them.' But it is not to be like that among you! Instead, whoever wants to be first shall be the slave of everyone. For the Son of Man did not come to be served, but to serve and to give his life as a ransom for many." 10:31 "Many who are first . . . will be last, and the last, first."	9:35 "If anyone wants to be first, let him be last of all and servant of everyone."

The Wisdom Myth	Wisdom of Solomon	Mark	Mark
	To you then, 0 monarchs, my words are directed, that you may learn wisdom and not transgress. For they will be made holy who observe holy things in holiness . . .		

Suggestions for Further Reading

Surveys of Literature on Mark's Gospel

Harrington, Daniel J. "A Map of Books on Mark (1975–1984)," *Biblical Theology Bulletin* 15:1 (1985), 12–16.

Humphrey, Hugh M. *A Bibliography for the Gospel of Mark 1954–1980.* Studies in the Bible and Early Christianity 1. New York/Toronto: Edwin Mellen Press, 1981.

Hurtado, LW. "The Gospel of Mark in Recent Study," *Themelios* 14:2 (1989), 47–52.

Kealy, Sean P. *Mark's Gospel: A History of Its Interpretation. from the Beginning Until 1979.* New York/Ramsey: Paulist, 1982.

Matera, Frank J. *What Are They Saying About Mark?* New York/Mahwah: Paulist, 1987.

Telford, William, ed. *The Interpretation of Mark.* Issues in Religion and Theology 7. Philadelphia/London: Fortress/SPCK, 1985.

On the Composition and Structure of the Gospel

Magness, J. Lee. *Sense and Absence. Structure and Suspension in the Ending of Mark's Gospel.* Semeia Studies. Atlanta: Scholars Press, 1986.

Stock, Augustine. *The Method and Message of Mark.* Wilmington: Michael Glazier, 1989.

van Iersel, Bas. *Reading Mark.* Translated by W.H. Bisscheroux. Collegeville: Liturgical Press, 1988.

Of Narrative and Story

Best, Ernest. *Mark. The Gospel as Story.* Studies of the New Testament and Its World. Edinburgh: T. & T. Clark, 1983.

_____ ."Mark's Narrative Technique," *Journal for the Study of the New Testament* 37 (1989), 43–58.

Rhoads, David, and Michie, Donald. *Mark as Story: An Introduction to the Narrative of a Gospel.* Philadelphia: Fortress, 1982.

About "Son of God" and "Wisdom"

Boring, M. Eugene. "The Christology of Mark: Hermeneutical Issues for Systematic Theology," *Semeia* 30 (1984), 125–153.

Humphrey, Hugh M. "Jesus as Wisdom in Mark," *Biblical Theology Bulletin* 19:2 (1989), 48–53.

Kingsbury, Jack Dean. *The Christology of Mark's Gospel.* Philadelphia: Fortress, 1983.

Mack, Burton L. "Wisdom Makes a Difference: Alternatives to 'Messianic' Configurations," *Judaisms and Their Messiahs at the Turn of the Christian Era.* Edited by Jacob Neusner et al. Cambridge/New York/New Rochelle/Melbourne/Sydney: Cambridge University, 1987, 15–48.

Marcus, Joel, "Mark 14:61: 'Are You the Messiah-Son of God?' " *Novum Testamentum* 31:2 (1989), 125–141.

About Response to Jesus in Mark

Beavis, Mary Ann, "Mark's Teaching on Faith," *Biblical Theology Bulletin* 16:4 (1986), 139–142.

Best, Ernest. *Disciples and Discipleship. Studies in the Gospel According to Mark.* Edinburgh: T. & T. Clark, 1986.

Malbon, Elizabeth Struthers, "Disciples/Crowds/Whoever: Markan Characters and Readers," *Novum Testamentum* 28:2 (1986), 104–130.

Marshall, Christopher D. *Faith as a Theme in Mark's Narrative.* Society for New Testament Studies Monograph Series 64. Cambridge/New York: Cambridge University Press, 1989.

Sweetland, Dennis M. *Our Journey with Jesus. Discipleship According to Mark.* Good News Studies 22. Wilmington: Michael Glazier, 1987.

On the Purpose or Social Setting of Mark

Lemcio, Eugene E. "The Intention of the Evangelist Mark," *New Testament Studies* 32:2 (1986), 187–206.

Stock, Augustine, "Chiastic Awareness and Education in Antiquity," *Biblical Theology Bulletin* 14:1 (1984), 23–27.

About Jewish Wisdom and the Wisdom of Solomon

Murphy, Roland E. *The Tree of Life.* The Anchor Bible Reference Library. New York/London/Toronto/Sydney/Auckland: Doubleday, 1990.

Winston, David. *The Wisdom of Solomon. A New Translation with Introduction and Commentary.* The Anchor Bible 43. New York/London/Toronto/Sydney/Auckland: Doubleday, 1979.

Index of Passages in Wisdom Literature

9:3–6, 25
9:5, 62, 64
9:9, 62
10:3, 10
10:4, 8
10:6, 9
10:9, 8
11:19, 9
16:2, 9
16:11, 9
17:2, 9
24:16, 9
25:28, 6
26:1–2, 6
26:27, 6

Sirach
1, 13, 157
1:1, 13
1:4, 13
1:6, 14
1:9–10, 14
1:11–20, 14
1:18–20, 14
2:15, 14
2:16, 14
2:16–18, 63
4:11, 14
4:12, 14
4:13, 14
4:16, 14
4:18, 14
4:19, 14
6:6–8, 14
6:19, 62
6:22, 14
6:26, 96
14:21–22, 96

15:1, 14
15:2–6, 14
15:3, 62, 64
21:19–21, 62
24, 13, 65, 157
24:3–9, 13
24:4, 13
24:5, 13
24:5–6, 64
24:8, 14
24:8–12, 62, 67
24:10–11, 113
24:10–14, 14
24:11, 101, 113
24:15–22, 14
24:19, 14
24:23, 14

Wisdom of Solomon
1:2–3, 39
1:6, 40
1:6–9, 39
1:7, 47
1:13, 16
1:16, 16, 33, 34, 141
1:16–2:12, 39
1:16–5:14, 16
2–5, 16
2:1, 34, 150
2:1–11, 16
2:1–5:16, 150
2:2–4, 150
2:5, 150
2:12, 33, 58, 149, 150, 153
2:12–5:8, 153
2:12–14, 33
2:12–16, 39